PAUL'S ETHIC OF FREEDOM

Paul's
Ethic of Freedom

BY
PETER RICHARDSON

THE WESTMINSTER PRESS
PHILADELPHIA

BOOK DESIGN BY DOROTHY ALDEN SMITH

First edition

Published by The Westminster Press®
Philadelphia, Pennsylvania

PRINTED IN THE UNITED STATES OF AMERICA
9 8 7 6 5 4 3 2 1

Library of Congress Cataloging in Publication Data

Richardson, Peter, 1935–
  Paul's ethic of freedom.

  Bibliography: p.
  Includes index.
  1. Bible. N.T. Epistles of Paul—Ethics.
2. Freedom (Theology)—Biblical teaching. I. Title.
BS2655.E8R5   241   78–27440
ISBN 0–664–24261–8

Dedicated to the memory of
GEORGE GRAINGER RICHARDSON
13 August 1904 to 28 January 1974

Contents

Preface

THIS FETUS has been a long time gestating, and longer than I should like in labor. Its origins go back, so far as I am conscious of them, to a young people's meeting sometime in the mid-1950's. It was on a Thanksgiving weekend, in the balcony of a Presbyterian Church in a small town in Ontario. We were being addressed by a minister, whose name I have long since forgotten, on the question of Christians drinking. It struck me from the texts that were quoted that there was a much more dramatic view of Christian freedom lurking in the—to me at the time—dim mists of Paul's letters than was being acknowledged. Twenty or so years later here is the result.

The immediate occasion for writing the book was a series of Wednesday evening studies with a group of Christians whom I have come to love and admire. They asked me to deal with Paul, partly because a talk I had given had helped to liberate some women in the congregation from their facile assumptions about their roles. So flattering was this that I could not resist the invitation. To St. Cuthbert's Presbyterian Church in Hamilton, Ontario, and to Paul McCarroll, I owe a great debt.

Several other debts should be acknowledged. Several times in my undergraduate teaching career at Loyola in Montreal (now part of Concordia University) I taught courses on "Authority, Freedom, and Anarchy." The students in those courses have shaped this material to some extent, even before it was contemplated as a book. But even more, some of the great writers who were discussed in those classes have influenced me, especially the Russian philosopher Nikolai Berdyaev. There may be few traces of it, but his book *Slavery and Freedom* has been a source of stimulus and delight. I am also indebted to students in a course at Scarborough College in the University of Toronto who read the material in an earlier draft and challenged, probed, and illuminated my view of Paul. Lastly I am grateful to Paul Gooch, my colleague there, who read and criticized the manuscript with grace and care.

G.P.R.

University College
University of Toronto

Introduction

THE MORE IMPORTANCE one gives to the idea of freedom in Paul's thought, the more difficulty one has in explaining early Christianity. Not only did the idea rather quickly and thoroughly disappear, but there was relatively little to account for the way freedom became a major category of thought for Paul. In Jesus' ministry the word seems almost totally absent, and so, to a large extent, is the idea. In Judaism obedience to the law—to Torah—assumes such a large place that freedom is much less highly valued. With Paul all this is turned around. Obedience to Torah is played down and freedom becomes an important conception. Yet none follows Paul in his stress on freedom.

Insofar as it seems to come from nowhere and to go nowhere, Paul presents us with something of a surd. How shall we account for him and how evaluate his significance? This study attempts to deal with these questions. It looks first of all at the roots of Paul's view of freedom, then at some of the specific features of its impact upon his ethics, then at some more general ethical principles, and lastly at how it worked out in the church. In developing this survey of Paul's attitude toward freedom, I have become increasingly persuaded that it is an important feature of his thought, developing out of his reflections on the Old Testament in the light of his convictions about Jesus and his experience of the Spirit. It is in the interaction of the Hebrew Scriptures with Jesus and the Spirit that his theology of freedom can best be situated.

It had little impact on succeeding generations because conditions changed, the needs that gave rise to Paul's views altered, and internal dissension and external threat required the church to turn its attention elsewhere.

I have relied heavily on the "great" letters of Paul: Galatians, I and II Corinthians, Romans. I rely somewhat less on the other letters that are generally accepted as Pauline: I and II Thessalonians, Philippians, Philemon, Colossians. Ephesians continues to come under attack as a Pauline letter; I am only too well aware of the force of these views, having difficulty making up my own mind on the question, but I include it here as Pauline. I leave to one side, for the most part, the pastoral letters—I and II Timothy and Titus. Unless otherwise noted all the translations are my own.

Every examination of Paul's letters must make some assumptions about when they were written and the circumstances under which they were written. Several schemes have been proposed, one of which seems to solve more problems and create fewer than the rest. The following order is presupposed in this study: Galatians; I and II Thessalonians; I Corinthians, chs. 10 to 13; II Corinthians, chs. 1 to 9; Philippians; Romans; Colossians; Philemon; Ephesians. In general I am not persuaded by the partition theories that have been proposed in recent years for several of the above. The subdivision of II Corinthians, though not crucial to the argument, is more compelling than any of the others. Absolute dates for each of the letters are not important for our purposes, but I imagine them all to have been written between A.D. 49 and 62.

I

Neither Jew nor Greek

IN THE MIDST of one of his most impassioned arguments about the law Paul makes a striking statement to the Galatians: "You are all children of God through faith in Christ Jesus, for as many of you as were baptized into Christ have put on Christ. There is neither Jew nor Greek, slave nor freeman, male nor female; for all of you are one in Christ Jesus. But if you are Christ's, then you are Abraham's seed and heirs of the promise." (Gal. 3:26ff.)

This is one of Paul's fundamental claims about the effects of faith in Jesus. Popular Jewish thought sets each half of the above pairs against the other; a traditional synagogue prayer states, "Lord, I thank you that you have not made me a barbarian, a slave, or a woman." The implications of this prayer are set aside by Paul because he believes that faith in Christ breaks down old oppositions and demands a new kind of oneness. What Jewish males thanked God for is now seen by Paul as totally inappropriate. It can hardly be accidental that Paul's statement develops the opposite view to that expressed in the prayer. He claims that the old antitheses are gone.

Paul's theoretical basis for this statement about Jew and Greek is in some measure established through his treatment of Abraham (see Gal., chs. 3 to 4). He goes back to Abraham as the father of Israel and develops the implications of the promise God made to him that he would be a blessing to all the nations of the earth. Paul also suggests that Abraham was himself the prototype for carrying out this promise: anyone who has Abraham's kind of faith can share in the blessing promised to Abraham. Thus the exclusiveness of Israel breaks down, according to Paul, right at the point where that exclusiveness began. The exclusiveness associated with Abraham is no longer considered by Paul to be valid.

In the second place, Paul claims that law, the most precious inheritance of the Jew which separates him from the non-Jew who has no access to God's particular revelation, was valid only until Christ had come. Afterward its force was dissipated and its role superseded. On both counts Paul's exegesis of the Hebrew Scriptures drives him to conclude that Jew and Greek (which he uses as shorthand for non-Jew or Gentile) are no longer to be divided as before (on law, see Rom., chs. 7 to 8; II Cor., ch. 3).

These theoretical assertions, however, did not solve the practical problems. The variety of persons found in the synagogues surrounding the Mediterranean, and even—though to a lesser extent—in Judea and Galilee, created even greater difficulty in the comparable Christian congregations. An ordinary congregation might be made up of Gentile Christians who had had no acquaintance with Judaism, God-fearing and proselyte Christians who had had some exposure to synagogue worship, Jewish Christians of various degrees of conservatism, some of whom would be Greek-speaking and some Aramaic-speaking. The mixture was explosive. We ought not to imagine that faith in Jesus as the Messiah solved all the problems that such a mixture could create.

The single most pressing issue in Paul's churches was the problem of the relationship of Jew and Greek. It was to this question he addressed himself most regularly, with numerous variations on a theme. Is there a priority connected with being a Jew? Can God go beyond Israel? Has God changed his mind? What is the status of the believing Gentile? And what is the relationship between the believing Gentile and the believing Jew? Between the believing Jew and the unbelieving Jew? Between the unbelieving Jew and the unbelieving Gentile? What are the ethical implications for Jews and Gentiles of a common belief in Jesus as Messiah? Can old traditions be assimilated to the new things that are happening through the Spirit in the time after Jesus?

Some of these questions will need to be raised later in connection with other facets of the problem of freedom. Here we shall describe the traditional exclusiveness of the people of God and Paul's response in terms of the freedom of God to do as he wills. The central point is that God's freedom is an important part of Paul's definition of Christian freedom. The major portions of this chapter will deal with Rom., chs. 1 to 3, and 9 to 11, but two other questions will be dealt with first: *(a)* the situation in Judaism before Paul and *(b)* the ways in which Paul's interest in the question of Jew and Greek rises and wanes.

1. JUDAISM BEFORE JESUS

It is common knowledge that Judaism claimed an exclusive relationship with God and hence a particular place in God's affections. The development of this view can be readily traced from God's dealing with Abraham (Gen. 12:3; 15:18ff.; 17:1–8; 17:15–23; 18:16–19; 21:1–13; 22:15–18; etc.). It continues on through the patriarchal developments, reaching an important turning point with God's reiteration of his promises to Moses (Ex. 3:6–12; 6:2–8). In the wilderness of Sinai, God reveals himself to Moses as Yahweh, the special name by which Israel henceforth knows him. He enjoins Israel to listen to him, to keep his covenant. If Israel is obedient, he says, "out of all peoples you shall become my special possession; for the whole earth is mine. You shall be my kingdom of priests, my holy nation" (Ex. 19:5–6). The law found in Ex., ch. 20, and the chapters following affirms Israel's special place before God. When the Decalogue begins "I am Yahweh your God . . ." (Ex. 20:2), it assumes the particular claims of Yahweh upon Israel and it sets out the appropriate response. This is reaffirmed in the Deuteronomic tradition (see, e.g., Deut. 28:9–14) and in the ancient Israelite historical records (Judges, Samuel, Kings). All of the material reinforces the contention that Israel is peculiarly God's; for its part Israel must abide by God's law, keep itself pure, and serve God only.

There is never any wavering from the view that Israel is exclusively God's own prized possession. Later there is set alongside it an expectation that in the future God will extend his blessing to include others. This is found most attractively in Second Isaiah (e.g., Isa. 56:6–8; 59:19–20; 60:1–14; 61:1–9; 66:18–24), but can be found in other parts of the prophetic tradition as well (e.g., Jonah 3:1–5; 4:10–11; Micah 4:1–7; 7:16–20; Zech. 14:16–19). In each case the wider expectation is a minor theme that fits within the hope of a reversal of Israel's fortunes. When Israel is restored to its rightful place, after its time of trial and punishment and separation from God, he will graciously draw a remnant to himself. In this future time, say some of the prophets, the nations will come to worship Yahweh at Mt. Zion; they too will share in Israel's worship. None of the prophets imagines that these other nations will be fully integrated into Israel; they share in true worship of God, but they do not become a part of his people.

In the literature written between the close of the Old Testament and the New Testament some of these same themes reemerge (e.g., II Esdras 7:37–38; Tobit 13:10–18 and in some manuscripts 13:6–9), but not in as highly developed a way as in some of the prophetic books. In II Esdras 1:22–37 a surprising, though tentative, statement is made to the effect that Israel will be abandoned, and the land of Israel will be handed over to a people who have not known God but who will do his bidding and receive his favor. "They shall perceive by the Spirit and believe all that I have said" (II Esdras 1:37, NEB). This idea remains undeveloped, and even in II Esdras its effect is modified by subsequent promises to Israel if they will repent and follow God. Much more usual in this period is the note of punishment on the nations because of the way they have trampled down Israel. This idea reaches a peak in the Qumran community's heightened sense of exclusiveness and its expectation of a decisive battle between the Sons of Light and the Sons of Darkness.

In spite of the weakness of the theme of the eschatological gathering of the nations of the earth to serve Yahweh at Mt. Zion, in fact many Gentiles did just that. During the intertestamental period Judaism increased its economic, cultural, and religious contacts with the other nations. The most important vehicle for doing so was the synagogue. As Jews spread around the shores of the Mediterranean and throughout the Middle East, taking their customs and culture and religion with them, many non-Jews learned enough of Israel and its God to find its worship attractive. Some became proselytes by accepting circumcision, some were content to go only part way toward incorporation into Israel. The ideal of the eschatological gathering of the nations at Mt. Zion was not developed, but in practice the nations were learning to follow Israel's God because of the Jews' dispersion throughout the rest of the world. Jesus' harsh saying about the scribes who crossed land and sea to make a single proselyte (Matt. 23:15) reflects this situation. It may be found also in statements of the rabbis about proselytes—for example, "when a

foreigner becomes a proselyte, one should stretch out a hand
to him to bring him under the wings of the Shekinah" (Lev.
R.2).

2. FROM JOHN TO PAUL

None of this strongly diminishes the sense of exclusiveness.
Gentiles must join Israel—become proselytes—to share in
the good things God has in store. God-fearers may get close
to Israel, but still do not share in all Israel's benefits. God is
bound to his long-standing commitments to his special people.

This view barely changes with John the Baptist or Jesus.
John states that God can raise up children for Abraham from
the stones (Matt. 3:9//Luke 3:8). Unfortunately we simply
do not have enough evidence to know in what ways John
might have developed this idea. Jesus only hints at a place for
Gentiles in God's purpose. We find these hints mostly in the
parables placed by the Gospel writers just before Jesus' death
(e.g., the cursing of the fig tree, Matt. 21:18–22//Mark 11:
12–14, 20–25; the two sons, Matt. 21:28–32; the vinedressers,
Matt. 21:33–46//Mark 12:1–12//Luke 20:9–19; the great
supper, Matt. 22:1–14; and the little apocalypse, Matt. 24:4–
36//Mark 13:5–37//Luke 21:8–36). For the most part, Jesus
retains a singularly Israel-centric concern, balanced on occasion by a broader appreciation of the Gentiles, and altered to
some extent by the resurrection sayings (especially Matt.
28:19–20). It is true that the writers of the Gospels, particularly Luke, show an increased concern for non-Jews in the
way they edit their Gospels, but this does not alter the essentially exclusive assumptions that Jesus shares with Israel as
a whole.

In the most primitive church there is evidence of a growing
concern for this problem. The book of The Acts, for example,

describes a number of important developments that take place prior to Paul's ministry. The account of the Day of Pentecost indicates that proselytes were a part of the crowd that day (Acts 2:10), and it quotes Joel 2:28–32 with its tentative universalist notions. Peter comments on that quotation by saying, "The promise is to you and to your children and *to all who are far off, to everyone* whom the Lord our God shall call" (Acts 2:39). Here is the record of a breakthrough, and it is important to note that the words are put in Peter's —not Paul's—mouth.

That there were some, perhaps many, conversions among proselytes and God-fearers visiting Jerusalem is very likely. It is certain that within the Jerusalem Christian community a split—or at least considerable tension—quickly developed between Aramaic- and Greek-speaking Christians. Acts 6:1 effectively describes the increasing numbers of disciples and reinforces the conclusion that the differences between the groups are important. The two groups of Christian widows are treated differently. To solve the problem, a group of Hellenistic (Greek-speaking) Christians were selected to assume some of the administrative responsibilities. The account goes on to imply that some of these also had a role to play in preaching and healing (Acts 6:8). Thus the end result was a widening division in Jerusalem between two groups of Christians, each with its own leadership. At least one of these leaders (Acts 6:5) was a proselyte, probably more were. Those who had been proselytes and God-fearers and were now Christians would naturally be associated with the Hellenistic group. Even in the early days of the church, and despite the theology of Peter's sermon on the Day of Pentecost, non-Jews were not fully assimilated into the Jewish Christian congregation in Jerusalem. Acts makes that a necessary conclusion.

Later, the persecution that followed the death of Stephen

forces Christians (almost certainly the *Hellenistic* Christians but not the Palestinian Christians) out of Jerusalem into Samaria (Acts 8:1ff.; 8:14; 8:25) and to other parts of the Mediteranean world (e.g., Philip in Acts 8:26ff.). In the course of this movement away from Jerusalem, Christianity reaches Damascus (Acts 9:1–2). We should not yet imagine that these first Christians have reached an understanding of the suitability of preaching to non-Jews. In almost every case the persons reached by the message are Jews or proselytes (note especially Acts 11:19ff.) or Samaritans who are related religiously to Judaism.

A turning point in the Acts narrative occurs in Luke's account of Cornelius the centurion. Cornelius is plainly described (Acts 10:1–2) as a God-fearer; the following account demonstrates the reality of his conversion to belief in Jesus as Messiah (e.g., Acts 10:44ff.). But the real significance of Luke's narrative lies in Peter's vision, the point of which is to persuade the leader of the Jerusalem Christians that old clean/unclean distinctions are superseded: "You yourselves know how unlawful it is for a Jew to associate with or to visit any one of another nation; but God has shown me that I should not call any man common or unclean" (Acts 10:28; cf. 10:15; 11:9; 11:17). The conclusion is represented by Luke as a dramatic turning point in early Christianity: "Then to the Gentiles also God has given repentance unto life" (Acts 11:18).

Without going into the details, we need to make reference to the so-called apostolic council, described in Acts, ch. 15. It was occasioned by a major difference of opinion, involving Paul and Barnabas (Acts 15:2) and presupposing considerable success in their mission to non-Jews. The specific problem was circumcision; Judean Christians were teaching, apparently, that "unless you are circumcised according to the custom of Moses you cannot be saved" (Acts 15:1; cf. 15:5). Paul and Barnabas were taking a different line. The council's decision, expressed through James, who seems by now to have replaced Peter as the leader of the Jerusalem church (Acts 15:13ff.), was that Gentiles can be accepted without being "troubled" by the demands of the law, though they should keep certain basic ethical requirements (15:20).

The situation was this. Early Christianity—i.e., before Paul's active ministry—had to grapple with the continuation of certain notions of exclusiveness. These exclusive tendencies are easily understood on the basis of Israel's past history. But within that history there is another later tradition that non-Jews will share in Israel's blessings. Unfortunately Jesus did not state his view on the matter unequivocally, and the church was beset with uncertainty over it. The tensions can readily be seen in the naming of the seven in Acts, ch. 6, and its aftermath. Luke's interest in the question can also be seen in the Cornelius incident. Luke intends for us to understand that through Cornelius' example and the decision of the council of Jerusalem an agreement has been reached that Gentiles can now be accepted readily. But it is hard to resist the conclusion that Luke has exaggerated the measure of agreement. Were Luke's view common, Paul would not have had the problems over Jew and Gentile of which his correspondence is evidence. We must conclude from the Pauline letters that for some Jewish Christians exclusiveness continued to be a major point of contention. The history of primitive Christianity continued to be troubled by a failure to reach a satisfying solution to the debate. One attempt at a fundamental solution is Paul's. That attempt is inextricably tied up with Paul's view of freedom.

3. Jew and Greek in Paul's Correspondence

The following survey of Paul's correspondence, in what should be close to the correct chronological order, will point up how Jewish exclusiveness and the entry of Gentiles clashed in Paul's churches. It will describe briefly the shape of the problem.

a. Galatians

An acute problem arose in the Galatian churches, perhaps just immediately prior to the apostolic council of Acts, ch. 15, through a conflict between Jewish and non-Jewish Christians. Some persons were "troubling" the Galatian Christians (Gal. 1:7), obviously over questions of circumcision (2:3; 2:12ff.; 2:21; 5:2,6,11; 6:12ff.). For Paul the root of the matter was the freedom that Christians have in Christ (2:4), a freedom that was confirmed by the Jerusalem apostles when they gave Paul and Barnabas the right hand of fellowship (2:7–9). According to Paul, freedom in Christ would be nullified if non-Jewish Christians were forced to accept circumcision (5:1ff.). Circumcision was being urged upon Gentile Christians not only by conservative Jewish Christians (and no doubt from Jews in Galatia, too) but also by Gentile Christians who had already been circumcised, probably as proselytes (6:13). Paul sarcastically suggests that the knife should have slipped and castrated them (5:12).

b. I Thessalonians

The Thessalonian Christians, predominantly Gentile in origin, were suffering persecution just as were the churches in Judea (I Thess. 2:14), as a result of the success of Paul's mission. Jews tried to prevent his preaching to Gentiles (2: 16), for Gentile acceptance of the good news was threatening.

Such success presaged the end (2:16), which was just around the corner (4:13ff.; 5:1ff.). It is possible that the connection which Paul made between Gentile acceptance, Jewish retribution, and the end was stimulated by refugees from Claudius' expulsion of the Jews from Rome reaching Thessalonica. Since the expulsion took place in A.D. 49, the chronology would fit. We know that the expulsion resulted from a riot over Chrestus (Christus?) and involved Christians as well (see Acts 18:2 and Suetonius, *Claudius* 25:4). A possible reconstruction is that Claudius was reacting to violent disputes within the Jewish and Christian community in Rome over the implications of Jesus Christ. If so, it is reasonable to infer that the disputes involved the questions of Gentile acceptance and the nearness of the end.

c. I Corinthians

The reception of the good news at Corinth still left numerous issues to disturb that unhappy congregation. One problem was circumcision. Paul's answer was that neither circumcision nor uncircumcision mattered, only keeping God's commandments (I Cor. 7:17–20). Another had to do with food offered to idols. Paul's answer was that liberty in food matters should not be pressed (8:4, 7–13; 10:23–30). Yet another was female participation in worship, perhaps understandable among Greeks but inevitably offensive to most Jews (11:2–16; 14:34–36). His view of the exercise of freedom within the relationship of Jews and Greeks is stated in 10:31 to 11:1: "Therefore whether you eat or drink or whatever you do, do everything unto God's glory. Be blameless to Jews and to Greeks and to the church of God, just as I also please everyone in everything, not seeking my own advantage, but that of many, in order that they should be saved. Become imitators of me, as I also am of Christ" (cf. also 12:13).

d. II Corinthians, chs. 10 to 13

The tensions in Corinth were still present, but the focus was almost entirely on the difficulties between Paul and other apostolic missionaries.

e. II Corinthians, chs. 1 to 9

There is an extended treatment in II Corinthians, chs. 8 to 9, of the collection for the poor saints in Jerusalem (mentioned also in other letters of this period, e.g., Gal. 2:10; I Cor. 16:1ff.; Rom. 15:25ff.; Phil. 4:14ff.). This collection was gathered from among largely Gentile churches and taken by a group of persons with Greek names (Acts 20:4) to the Jewish congregations in Judea. It is likely that the purpose of this offering was to demonstrate to Jews the correctness of the decision to allow Gentiles into the fellowship without laying other burdens on them. Their admission demonstrated God's intention to save all flesh. The representative group of Gentiles who brought the gift was a small fulfillment of the eschatological gathering of the Gentiles to worship God on Mt. Zion. So Paul's ministry was vindicated. When Paul and his friends reached Jerusalem with the money (Acts 21:17ff.), they were received gladly, though not without reservations on the part of some (Acts 21:20ff.). It is ironic in the extreme that Paul's willingness to accede to the request of James and others to prove his continued faithfulness to Judaism led to his arrest, his voyage to Rome, and his death.

f. Philippians

Chapter 3 is testimony to the extent of the difficulties posed in a Pauline congregation by the variety of Christians and Jews present. In Philippi as in Corinth and to a lesser extent in Thessalonica, some have been influenced by incipient gnosticizing ideas (see Chapter V). The animosity, for whatever reasons, that is presupposed in the harsh statements about Jews (Phil. 3:2) shows how little the basic problem was solved.

g. Romans

This circular letter deals most fully with the relationship, both practical and theoretical, between Jews and Greeks. We shall examine it in detail shortly.

h. Colossians (and Philemon)

By the time Colossians was written the possibility of a straightforward conflict between Jews and Greeks within a Christian congregation had receded. God had revealed "among the Gentiles" the glory of the mystery of Christ (Col. 1:27). Circumcision was viewed for the first time as an analogy to baptism (Col. 2:11ff.), and feasts and other regulations were merely a shadow of what was to come (Col. 2:16f., 21ff.). The older Galatians' formula—neither Jew nor Greek —is here repeated (Col. 3:11) but without the male/female antithesis! The acute problem in Colossians was not Jew and Greek, but the pressing conflict with a gnosticizing Jewish Christianity over the nature of the person of Jesus.

i. Ephesians

If this letter was written by Paul, it represents a further stage away from a concern for the relationship of Jew and Greek. The real difference between those who come to Jesus from a Jewish background and those who come from a Gentile background (as in Galatians, I Corinthians, and Romans, and even I Thessalonians) is totally submerged (e.g., Eph. 2:3). In Eph. 2:11–22 it is evident that Gentiles have assumed a dominant role in the church: they were uncircumcised, separated, without hope, but now are brought near, reconciled, and are part of the new temple. In short, the dividing wall of hostility is broken down (Eph. 2:14).

From these brief indications of the varying ways in which Jew and Gentile were treated by Paul we may draw several preliminary conclusions of some importance:

(1) The problem of Jew and Greek affected primarily, but not exclusively, Pauline churches. This was so because of Paul's singular sense of mission to the Gentiles and his heavy emphasis on a gospel of freedom in Christ. This combination —churches predominantly Gentile in origin and a stress on freedom from Mosaic law and Jewish tradition—created an explosive situation if Jews within the congregation had a sensitive conscience.

(2) Paul handled this as a pastoral problem except in The Letter to the Romans. Possibly because he had no pastoral relationship to that congregation in Rome, he developed a strong theoretical basis for his view.

(3) The tensions eased as time went on, not because the problem was solved but because new Christians increasingly came from Gentile ranks.

(4) The suggestion that the Gentiles' acceptance of the good news meant that the end—with its great eschatological ingathering—was near eventually failed to convince. Jews did not flock to the church as a result of Paul's collection.

(5) With Paul's arrest and with the continuation of the "present age," his concerns shifted increasingly to the questions posed by the growing dominance of the Gentiles within the church.

4. ROMANS, CHS. 1 TO 3: THERE ARE NO DISTINCTIONS

With this survey of the Jewish background, the developments in the earliest church, and the course of Paul's correspondence we may now turn to the one place where he deals at length with the set of problems posed in the middle fifties by the tensions between Jew and Greek.

The introductory greetings note that Paul's apostleship is to bring about "obedience to faith among all the nations" (Rom. 1:5). The thanksgiving, beginning in v. 8, indicates that Paul wishes to reap some harvest among the Romans and the rest of the Gentiles, because he is under obligation to Greeks and to barbarians (Rom. 1:13–14; cf. also Rom. 15:18; Gal. 2:7,9). It was not a casual decision, therefore, to establish as the theme for this letter, repeated often in what follows, "to the Jew first and also to the Greek" (Rom. 1:16). Even though both he and the Jerusalem apostles viewed his ministry as directed to Gentiles (cf. also Acts 15:7), Paul still gave a priority to Jews in The Letter to the Romans. This priority was both logical and chronological. *(a)* Jesus and his disciples were all Jews; *(b)* his ministry was almost exclusively to Jews; *(c)* the foundation churches were Jewish; *(d)* the major apostles (perhaps all) were Jewish.

Paul's own practice, following this logic, was to go to the Jews first (Acts 13:4, 14; 14:1; 16:13; 17:1,10,17; 18:4,19; 19:8). It was important that they hear. But from the rest of Romans it would appear that this was a necessary priority, for Paul assumed that the Jews' rejection of the good news would free him to go to Gentiles.

As we shall see, though Paul felt duty bound to acknowledge a priority to Jews, this priority conflicted with his primary ministry to Gentiles (Gal. 2:7) and it tended in the direction of a traditional Jewish exclusivism which he wished to reject. His handling of these problems was not completed until he reached his brilliant proposals in Rom., chs. 9 to 11.

The statement of his basic thesis, "To the Jew first and also to the Greek," is followed in Rom. 1:17 by a repetition of that verse from Hab. 2:4 (cited also in Gal. 3:11) which is so seminal for Paul. The good news saves, he says, because in it the righteousness of God is revealed through (or by) faith unto faith, as Habakkuk anticipated. Romans, chs. 1 to 3, is the working out of the first stage of this theme.

The opening shot is fired in Rom. 1:18–31. It is aimed at men generally who, apart from special revelation, have a general knowledge of God. That knowledge, says Paul, is enough to render all men without excuse (1:19–20); the behavior described in the rest of the chapter is viewed as the obvious working out of a refusal to act on that knowledge (1:18,21,25,28,32). The argument is taken a step further in 2:1–11, though it is not clear who "the man" addressed in this paragraph is. It could be the moral pagan who looks with disdain on those who are less moral than he; it could be the Jew (in anticipation of 2:17ff.) who frowns on even the best Greek morality. In either case, God's judgment (2:1–5) will be rendered on the basis of behavior (2:6–9). So there will be "tribulation and calamity upon every human being who produces evil—the Jew first and also the Greek—but glory and honor and peace to all who produce good—the Jew first and also the Greek" (2:9–10). This surprising conclusion is reinforced by the final phrase of this paragraph: "There is no favoritism with God" (2:11). If the Old Testament is to be believed, God *does* show favoritism. He selected Israel from all the nations of the world, he revealed to Israel his way, he poured out his mercy and grace upon it, and even though Israel frequently went astray, God always promised future blessing. Here, in a discussion of all people, Paul concludes that punishment and praise will be bestowed impartially, though to the Jew first (both calamity and praise) and then to the Greek. Paul begins to diverge from his more conservative Jewish compatriots.

He develops this idea further in 2:12–16, still in the context of judgment (v.16), once again making some surprising moves. Those who sin outside of law will perish outside of law; those who sin under law will be judged by the law (v.12).

What matters is doing the law (2:13). So Gentiles may by
nature do what the law requires, without having the law,
because the law is written on their hearts (2:14–15). As in II
Cor., ch. 3, Paul here betrays considerable meditation on the
postexilic traditions about the new heart given to man. But
in Romans he has reapplied this idea and has thereby set up
an alternative to the exclusively Jewish knowledge of God
through the law.

This daring development is followed by a thinly veiled
accusation against Jews (2:17–24). A Jew will rely on the law
and his relationship with God (2:17). But a high degree of
knowledge makes a high demand for consistency (2:18–22),
so if one boasts in the law, one must not break the law (2:23).
Then follows his accusation, drawn from Isa. 52:5 possibly
mixed with Ezek. 36:20–21, that because of God's people, the
Gentiles blaspheme God's name (the idea itself is not present
in Isaiah but is somewhat similar in the Ezekiel reference).

This leads Paul to deal with an obvious objection: Then
what value is circumcision? Does it not establish a person's
relationship with God? The answer is by now common; it is
of value if you keep the law, but it becomes uncircumcision,
almost equivalent to "like a Gentile," if you do not (Rom.
2:25). The most obvious background for this logic is found
in Jer. 9:25–26 (cf. Jer. 4:4), where Israel's being uncircumcised in heart is likened to the state of the surrounding nations—Egypt, Judah, Edom, Ammon, Moab—who are all
circumcised yet uncircumcised. Stephen too used this logic
(Acts 7:51). From this Old Testament analogy Paul argues,
with a new degree of daring, that the uncircumcised person
who keeps the law will be considered circumcised.

Previous to Romans he argued only that circumcision or
uncircumcision doesn't matter (thus Gal. 5:6 and I Cor.
7:19). He now concludes, perhaps with Deut. 30:6 in the back
of his mind, that "he is not a Jew who is one outwardly, nor

is circumcision the outward kind, but the Jew is the hidden
one and circumcision is of the heart, in spirit, not letter"
(Rom. 2:28–29). This elliptical thought needs to be completed with the idea of "true" or "real"; neither of the words
is used in this sentence, though the meaning is clear enough.
Circumcision is not outward; it is inward, spiritual, and deals
with the heart. Paul's reserve in his manner of expression
(why did he not say "true Jew"?) contrasts with his innova-
tive intention.

The fat is now in the fire. Paul raises the general question
about the possible advantage of being a Jew (Rom. 3:1). He
raises this question again a few verses later, but this first time
he answers it unequivocally: there is much value in being
Jewish. His use of "first" (3:2) indicates that he intends to
enumerate several advantages. He gets no farther than to
name one: the "oracles" or "messages" of God were en-
trusted to the Jew. A digression follows based on a real or
imagined objection that Paul's view is inadequate if some
Jews are unfaithful to those oracles (3:3–8).

Since his first attempt is deflected he asks the question
rhetorically again. This time Paul asks and answers it quite
ambiguously. The question can be translated either, "Are we
at an advantage?" or, "Are we at a disadvantage?" and the
answer can be translated either, "Not at all" or, "Not completely." Given the connection with the preceding, it seems
best to translate it: "Are we then worse off? Not at all." If
so, Paul begins by allowing for a Jewish advantage and then
rejects the view that the Jew is at a disadvantage. The reason
for this is that all—both Jews and Greeks—are under sin
(3:9), as demonstrated by a series of Scripture quotations
drawn from the Psalms and Isaiah. This all sounds very
much like a set piece hammered out in his missionary preaching to mixed audiences of Jews and Greeks: there are no
distinctions.

Paul's classic formulation of justification by faith now fits in (3:21–26). Since there are no distinctions (3:22), both are dealt with alike by God. Jewish behavior can cut a Jew off from God's blessing, and Gentile behavior can bring a Gentile into God's blessing. All have sinned; whoever is justified is justified by his grace through redemption which occurs in Christ Jesus (3:24). It all rests on the basis of faith in Jesus (3:26), who is an expiation for sin (3:25).

The application of this argument must be worked out explicitly. God is not just the God of the Jews, he is also the God of the Gentiles, for there is only one God (3:28f.). He justifies the circumcised on the basis of faith and the uncircumcised through faith (3:30). Therefore no Jew can boast (3:27).

At this point Paul has demonstrated to his satisfaction that Jew and Greek are treated alike before God; each enters into a relationship with God only on the basis of faith. But what is the significance of this assertion of Paul's? He has transcended his inherited assumptions about God's relationship to Israel. The old exclusive view of Israel's role is superseded in favor of a radical revision prompted by his deep concern to understand what God is doing in his day. His view of God's freedom, which emerges more clearly in chapters 9 to 11, prompts him to see new ways for God to work not previously seen, and all because of his conviction that what has happened in Jesus is new.

5. ROMANS, CHS. 9 TO 11: GOD'S FREEDOM

Paul's argument moves from the conclusion that God makes no distinctions because he justifies by faith in Jesus, to a treatment of Abraham (4:1), of sin (6:1), and of law (7:7). He then returns in 9:1 to the questions dealt with in chs. 1 to 3, but at a different level.

His expression of anguish in 9:1–3 picks up his concern in 3:1 and 3:10 about the possibility of a Jewish advantage. The advantage could be found in Israel's sonship (or adoption?), glory, covenants, law, worship, promises, patriarchs, and even the Messiah. In fact, the position of Israel is precarious (9:4–5).

To unpack the implications of this argument, he first lays out his assumptions about God's freedom (9:6–13). In doing so, he develops his earlier Abraham theme with respect to Isaac and Jacob/Israel (9:6–10). He goes beyond what he said earlier in ch. 4 when he claims (9:11–12) that God freely chooses a particular line of descent in order to demonstrate that grace is at his discretion and cannot be manipulated or presumed upon. This choice may sound almost capricious, but that is not what Paul is trying to say. He is wrestling with the historical-biological fact that not all of Abraham's children are children of God, for Edom and Moab also can trace their antecedents through Esau to Abraham, and Judaism is sure that they are far from God. So Paul proposes a *theological* reason for this: God selected Jacob instead of Esau in order to show that his own initiative in the process is of inestimably more importance than works. This is dramatically evident in this case because the choice by God took place before the twins were born.

This is unjust (9:14), says an opponent. To this Paul replies that God revealed to Moses his basic principle of freedom, that he shows mercy and compassion to whom he wishes (9:15, drawn from Ex. 33:19 whose context is Moses' meeting with God and needing to veil his face!). Everything depends upon God's mercy, not on human will or effort (9:16).

Paul deals with another objection in 9:19–24, developing Scriptural warrant for his views from Hosea and Isaiah, and concluding that justice is served even if only a remnant is saved (9:27–28).

With this Paul moves to a crucial new phase in his logic. Gentiles have not ordinarily pursued righteousness, but they have found it through faith. Israel pursued it through law and could not attain it (9:30–32; cf. almost the same thought in 10:1–3). This failure occurs, he says, because "Christ is the end of the law unto righteousness to everyone who believes" (10:4).

Believing or trusting comes through preaching that Jesus is the Lord who has been raised from the dead. Since all have the same opportunity to respond, and since Scripture has promised that "whoever believes will not be put to shame" (quoting the Greek translation of Isa. 28:16), there can be no distinction between Jew and Greek: "Everyone who calls on the name of the Lord will be saved" (10:13, quoting Joel 2:32).

With this the first half of his argument in chs. 9 to 11 is completed. His main points are:

(1) That he has found in practice what he knew in theory, that God is free to call whom he chooses;
(2) That he has found also in his own experience that all of God's people never respond wholeheartedly to God's call, as he already knew from the Old Testament;
(3) That in God's calling, everyone who attains righteousness does so because of faith;
(4) Hence, that there can be no distinction between Jew and Greek.

From here to the end of ch. 11, Paul is preoccupied with one concern: Why? Why has God allowed Israel to reject his message of preaching? Why have the Gentiles appeared to accept it so eagerly? Paul's reasoning on this reveals important features of his view of the relationship between Jew and Gentile (for a fuller treatment, see my *Israel in the Apostolic*

Church, 1969, pp. 126–147). His argument may be broken down into the following stages:

a. Preaching is the way God calls people; this preaching is now going on in the ministry of Paul and others (10:14–18).

b. Gentiles have understood and are accepting, but Israel seems uninterested. To judge from Deut. 32:21, God will stir up Israel and make it jealous of the Gentiles (10:19–21). *This is the key to what follows.*

c. Even though Israel behaves badly, God always retains a remnant (11:1–6) which obtains what Israel is looking for (11:7–10).

d. According to Paul, Israel's sin allows God to grant salvation to Gentiles, but only in order to make Israel itself jealous (11:11). This is completely consistent with Paul's starting point: "To the Jew first and also to the Greek." In 11:12 he even envisages Israel's "full inclusion."

e. Paul now speaks to the Gentiles to remind them that Israel will become jealous and so accept (11:13–16).

f. For a fourth time Paul develops the same approach using the metaphor of the olive tree (a standard symbol for Israel). Just as God prunes some branches off and grafts some alien branches on, so he can clip off the grafted branches and graft on the old pruned branches (11:17–24)! Any simple view of God's action is inadequate. God works in complex ways.

g. Some Gentiles in Rome are congratulating themselves on taking the place of the Jews in God's affections and are claiming a priority. Paul warns them not to boast about Israel's hardening (11:25; cf. 11:18); it will last only until the full number of Gentiles come in, and then all Israel will be saved (11:26).

h. Once more he repeats the same thought in different terms, in a neatly structured summary of his thought so far (11:28–32).

v. 28a As regards the gospel, enemies for your sake;

v. 28b as regards election, beloved for the patriarchs' sake.

v. 29 For the gifts and the call of God are irrevocable.

v. 30 For just as you once were disobedient to God, but now have received mercy in this disobedience,

v. 31 so also they now have been disobedient for your mercy, so that now they may receive mercy.

v. 32 For God has consigned all to disobedience in order to have mercy on all.

This is the most precise form of Paul's thesis: Israel is both beloved and enemy. Since God's call is irrevocable, it is impossible that Israel will remain opposed to God. Its disobedience means mercy to the Gentiles, but Israel will still be recipient of God's mercy ultimately. In the great paean of praise in 11:33–36 Paul hints that God's ways and judgments are not to be discerned completely, his wisdom and knowledge exceed man's by so much. But great satisfaction may be gained from the certainty that "from him and through him and unto him are all things."

6. CONCLUSION

Paul began by stating that God's righteousness, made known through the good news, is for the Jew first and also the Gentile. He demonstrates the desperate condition of the Gentile, then of the Jew, and shows how both may escape judgment by God's goodness. The Jew's assumption of exclusiveness, and the Gentile's plight apart from God, are both transcended by God, who can turn circumcision into uncir-

cumcision and uncircumcision into circumcision. God no
longer distinguishes on that basis: all have sinned, all may be
justified by the grace that is made evident in Jesus Christ.

However, Israel's priority is still real and God's election of
Israel cannot be set to one side, even though Israel itself must
not depend on it for salvation. The law is not adequate,
otherwise God's freedom to call either Jew or Greek would
be restricted.

Two sides to Israel's election still remain: *(a)* As the Old
Testament demonstrates, God has always retained a remnant, and he still does so. *(b)* In a totally new vein, it is only
because of Israel's temporary rejection that Gentiles can hear
and accept the message. This will make Israel jealous and
ultimately the rejection of the people of Israel will be re-
versed, so that they too shall be saved.

So Paul both retains and denies Israel's special place in
God's scheme of things. He looks forward with confidence to
the *eschaton,* when the full number of Jews will be present.
For the present, God exercises his freedom by moving beyond Israel's exclusive relationship with him so that he can
call both Jews and Gentiles to him on the basis of faith in
Jesus—Jew first and also Greek.

With this argument Paul works out the first clause of his
programmatic statement in Gal. 3:28: in Christ there is neither Jew nor Greek. This pressing question had to be faced
or Gentile Christians would either have been left as second-
class citizens or have become totally assimilated. Paul attempted to preserve the freedom of Gentile Christians to
continue to be *Gentiles* by arguing from the freedom of God
to call whom he wills. The argument was ultimately successful, even if it was not immediately persuasive to other seg-
ments of the fledgling church.

The church today no longer faces the same Jew and Greek
issue that it once did. But two related problems arise. The

first is the continuing, though submerged, question of the attitude of Christians toward Jews. Anti-Semitism is still alive, as too many incidents reported in our newspapers demonstrate. Though neither Paul nor other New Testament writers were anti-Semitic, the church rather quickly developed an anti-Jewish view that formed the basis for what later became anti-Semitism. The second problem is the matter of insiders and outsiders. Paul's way of dealing with the inclusion of Gentiles is suggestive for our approach to the inclusion of other identifiable minorities.

II

Neither Slave nor Free

PAUL WROTE to the Galatians that in Christ there is neither slave nor freeman. We might expect him to work out the implications of this motif, as he did with the Jew/Greek question, but he did not. It is disconcerting to us, with our twentieth-century assumptions and convictions, that he is so relaxed about slavery. He never deals with the sense of exclusiveness that being a freeman conveys to a person in the Hellenistic world. He has, fortunately, left us a letter that has slavery as the immediate background, and to Philemon we shall turn in due course. He also makes other comments about slavery and freedom. But the bare fact remains that Paul never once comments on slavery as an institution. So, though we have a good bit of his correspondence he leaves us in doubt about what it might mean for a slave to become a Christian.

This creates an awkward situation. If we take seriously Paul's interest in freedom, and if we acknowledge his concern to break down the barrier between Jew and Greek, how can we accept his apparent indifference to the barrier between free and slave? Why does he not go further in asserting slaves' freedom? There are two dangers in attempting to respond to that question. On the one hand, we might neglect the huge differences between our culture and his. On the other hand, we might exaggerate the possible excuses for Paul's hesitancy about slavery.

The differences between the twentieth century and the first century are too obvious to be detailed. Slavery was an accepted institution, not only in Hellenistic civilization and more extensively in the whole Near East but also within Biblical law. The ills of slavery were real, but were not so obviously ills as they seem to us. Paul's acceptance of slavery as an institution is at least partly cultural, like our acceptance of the cold war, the energy crisis, and the income tax.

Even acknowledging the differences, which will be more apparent when slavery in the ancient world is described, we might still expect the incisive and imaginative Paul to attack the subjection of one person to another. The eventual elimination of slavery was based upon Biblical views on human personality, freedom, and dignity, and upon the hints contained in Paul's letters. But Paul himself never drew the conclusions that the nineteenth-century legislators drew from the same material. There might be a number of reasons for Paul's hesitancy, in addition to the cultural differences.

First, for most of his career Paul anticipated that the end would come soon, ushered in by the *parousia* of Jesus. This would contribute to his social conservatism. When Paul deals with slavery in his later correspondence he seems to have become even more conservative than he was earlier, probably because of the developing danger of radicalism (see Chapters III and V).

Second, Paul felt that social institutions as institutions did not deserve first attention. He was interested in relationships, and the effects of the chasm between freeman and slave could be bridged by the quality of personal and corporate relationships when both were "in Christ." The reason he was so interested in the Jew/Greek question is that a failure to resolve it would result in two separate churches, an intolerable contradiction for Paul. The same threat did not attach to the slave/free problem.

Third, Paul was not personally engaged with the slave/free question as he was with the Jew/Greek set of issues. The differences between him and the Jerusalem apostles, his self-identification as an apostle to the Gentiles, his own concern over the role of law and circumcision made it personally imperative for him to deal with the abolition of the distinction between Jew and Greek. There was not the same pressure to resolve questions about slavery, nor about females (see Chapter III).

Personal involvement and priorities, even more than cultural and theological factors, prevented Paul from dealing fully or straightforwardly with the question of freedom and slavery.

1. SLAVERY IN JUDAISM

As a Jew, Paul inherited the Biblical legacy of slavery. In the Pentateuch the acceptance of slavery is a part of the general custom of slavery within the Near Eastern world. Economically and socially integral to Judaism, slavery had deep roots in the legal provisions of the Pentateuch. Though it is difficult to be certain how those provisions may have been modified by rabbinic interpretation before Paul's time, we may be tolerably certain that there was no likelihood that slavery within Judaism would cease.

Legally slaves were chattels, completely at the service and discretion of their owner. They might be well- or ill-treated, but apart from the right to do grievous bodily harm (which would result in freedom for the slave), the owner was the judge of his own actions. Female slaves too were at the discretion of the master, to be used sexually or given to others for sexual use if one wanted. They might be seen as a way of breeding more slaves, or as concubines, or even as prostitutes. However, a female slave who bore a child for her mistress' husband could not be sold; this is a part of the background to the incident in which Hagar and Ishmael are sent away by Abraham and Sarah (Ex., ch. 16; cf. Deut. 21:14 for an alien female slave).

Judaism distinguished carefully between Hebrew slaves and alien slaves. The latter might be born into slavery or come as captives in war (Deut. 20:10ff.) or through slave traders; the former would come through the selling of thieves to make restitution (Ex. 22:1) or through a person selling himself because of insolvency (Lev. 25:39; Amos 2:6).

The Hebrew slave, male or female, was to be released after six years of service (Ex. 21:2; Deut. 15:12) and given compensation for service rendered. According to Lev. 25:40, slaves were to be released in the first jubilee year. There were other grounds for release as well; for example, a female slave who had been sold on the understanding that she would be married to the master's son was to be set free if he defaulted on that or some other provision (Ex. 21:7–11). By contrast, the service of aliens was not to be terminated, and slavery passed on from parents to children (Lev. 25:44–46). In general there was allowance in the Near East for a slave to be manumitted (freed) by purchase of freedom, but there did not seem to be any provision in Israel for this practice except for Hebrew slaves (Lev. 25:47–52).

All slaves became members of an Israelite's household. Aliens were circumcised so they could then share in numerous features of Israel's life and worship. Without that, ordinary family life would be rendered impossible for a strict Jew. Jewish slaves were in a much more favorable position than Gentile slaves, and were spared some of the more humiliating jobs. If there were some degree of kindness extended to both Israelite and alien slaves, it was motivated to a large extent by the constant recollection that Israel had been a slave in Egypt. Out of the remembered agony of that experience, Israel's own institution of slavery was applied in such a way that some religious and social rights were given to slaves. They became a part of the family, and members of Israel. Granted the basic premise, the institution of slavery seems to have been applied in a reasonably humane way.

2. SLAVERY IN THE HELLENISTIC AND ROMAN WORLDS

Though slavery was accepted uncritically in Jewish society, it was not as essential to Israel as it was to Greece and Rome. In the Near East, slaves constituted a minority of the population, in the Greco-Roman world a large majority. To abolish slavery would have altered essentially the fabric of Greek society and changed both the understanding of labor and the opportunity for leisure.

In the Hellenistic world, slavery could result from capture in war or piracy; this applied both to male combatants and to women and children from captured cities. But the numbers required could never be provided by even the most successful wars. The major supply came from slave dealers, usually dealing in slaves from the north and the east. The slave dealers, some of whom followed the armies and dealt in the slaves that became available through war, were thus important traders in the economy. In addition to these sources, children were often sold into slavery, providing yet another inexpensive supply. So the large quantity of slaves that was important to Greek civilization could be supplied relatively cheaply and easily. As a result of this traffic in slaves some cities acquired a reputation as major slave markets. Until the first century B.C., and perhaps even later, Ephesus was a major center for slave trade.

The scale of slavery was vast. The numbers of slaves might

have amounted to anywhere from three to five times the number of citizens in the state, though such calculations are imprecise, and vary from state to state and from time to time. With the increasingly pervasive presence of Rome in the Mediterranean world, the demand for slaves increased still more. Rome became the major destination of slave traffic, and the sources shifted more and more to Asia Minor and the East. The commercial consequences of slavery were so great, according to Rostovtzeff, that in the reorganization of Rome's economic life the slave trade was a fundamental feature. The extent of slavery was, if anything, increasing in the century before the beginning of Christianity.

The slave revolts of the first century B.C. (popularized by the movie *Spartacus*) are a dramatic though often exaggerated indication of the scope of the problems posed by slavery. The revolts were not usually successful, nor did they have serious effects on Roman culture. Their significance lies mainly in the fact that tremendous difficulties had to be overcome to organize a slave revolt. The successful beginning of a revolt therefore speaks volumes about the conditions that created them.

A continuing problem was distressingly common: the flight of individual slaves from their masters. This condition is obviously reflected in the little letter to Philemon. Our knowledge of fugitives is not restricted to that letter. There exists also a papyrus document (from about 150 B.C.) containing a notice about two slaves who had run away, which reads in part as follows:

The servant of Aristogenes the son of Chrysippus, an ambassador of Alabanda, has run away. Name, Hermon, *alias* Nilus, Nationality, Syrian, of Hierapolis. Age, about 18, of medium height, clean shaven, sturdy in the leg, with a dimple in the chin, a mole on the left of the nose, a scar above the left corner of the mouth, tattooed on the right wrist. . . . Anybody bringing him back will receive 2 talents in bronze; for indicating that he is in asylum at a temple, 1 talent; for indicating that he is with a substantial person who is subject to the law, 3 talents. And anybody writing to give information may do so to the governor's representatives. There is also one Bion, the slave of Callicrates . . .

A similar situation, though concerning a freedman, is presupposed in a letter from the younger Pliny to a friend (Pliny, *Epistles,* ix.21; about A.D. 108):

Your freedman, with whom you had told me you were vexed, came to me, and throwing himself down before me clung to my feet, as if they had been yours. He was profuse in his tears and his entreaties. . . . You are angry, I know; and you have reason to be angry, this I also know: but mercy wins the highest praise just when there is the most righteous cause for anger. . . . Do not torture him, lest you torture yourself at the same time.

The occasional flight of slaves was not threatening for financial so much as for social reasons. Escaped slaves who were not caught and returned posed a threat to the fabric of society because their remaining at liberty would act as an incentive to the runaway's fellows to follow suit. The instability created might become intolerable.

Other forms of dissent and disobedience were known, the most extreme being the slave who rose against his master and killed him. A famous case is cited by Tacitus (*Annals,* xiv.42; about A.D. 61), in which a senator was killed. The law required that every slave in the household should be executed. The senate took this case under advisement as a result of a popular outcry. A speech by C. Cassius is reported as follows:

The dispositions of slaves were regarded with suspicion by our ancestors, even when they were born on the same estates or in the same houses and learned to feel an affection for their masters from the first. Now, however, when we have several nations among our slaves, with various rites, with foreign religions or none at all, it is not possible to keep down such a rabble except by fear.

As a result, four hundred slaves were executed. But it is interesting that popular feeling was sufficiently in favor of the slaves to call for the senatorial examination. Sentiment could work on behalf of slaves. Nevertheless, slavery in the Hellenistic world was an oppressive institution, shot through with fear, malice, and resentment on both sides. The popular proverb, "As many enemies as slaves" (quoted by Seneca, *Moral Epistles,* 47), contains more than one truth.

3. PHILEMON AND ONESIMUS

Paul's attitude toward slavery was undoubtedly affected by all of this. On the one hand, he was a Jew and Judaism accepted slavery, though that form of slavery was less extensive and less exploitative than the Hellenistic form. On the other hand, one of the foundations of the economic system of the world in which Paul worked was slavery, and to encourage radical change could add to the disorder of an already alienated world. So, while change might be welcomed, it was not openly advocated.

The institution of slavery forms a necessary part of the background to this little letter. Paul had met Onesimus, one of the many runaway slaves, while under a loose form of arrest in Rome (cf. Acts 28:16, 30f.). Since Paul was not "in prison" but "in bonds" (Philemon 10), it is not likely that he had met Onesimus in prison. Had Onesimus been in prison, as is usually suggested, he would simply have been shipped back to suffer whatever punishment his master, Philemon, cared to hand out, up to and including death. This may mean, then, that Paul was sheltering Onesimus, and that could throw a very different light on the situation. If Philemon was a Roman citizen, Paul, as a fellow Roman, would be guilty of a serious offense subject to a penalty of double the slave's value.

With Onesimus on his hands, Paul writes to Philemon and to the church that meets in his house. After conventional greetings and a thanksgiving (Philemon 1–7), Paul gets to the point: his appeal on behalf of Onesimus. But, as compared with Pliny's letter quoted earlier in which the request was plain and straightforward, the appeal here to Philemon is opaque and convoluted:

> Though I could command . . . I prefer to appeal. . . . I appeal for my child. . . . I am sending him back. . . . I wanted to keep him. . . . I preferred to do nothing without your consent . . . so if you consider me as your partner, receive him as you would me. If he has wronged you . . . I will repay it. . . . I know you will do even more than I say. (Philemon 8–20)

The request is never quite made. Does Paul want Philemon simply to take Onesimus back as a slave? To give him the minimum punishment? To set him free? To cancel some debt? To send Onesimus back for Paul's use? The one thing that is clear is that Paul puts the onus on Philemon for receiving Onesimus back as a brother, now that Onesimus has become a Christian. This is good counseling, perhaps, but it leaves us questioning Paul's attitude toward slavery.

Why should Paul not have asked outright that Onesimus be freed? Or why not force Philemon's hand by sending along the purchase price, instead of asking him to chalk up Onesimus' debts to Paul's accounts? Or why did he not say that one Christian ought not to own another?

Even though the situation itself cannot be exactly reconstructed, we do know of an Onesimus who, toward the end of the first century, became a bishop in Ephesus. Could he be the same person? If so, and it is by no means certain, Philemon must have freed Onesimus. What is more, the runaway slave would have risen to high ecclesiastical office.

Be that as it may, in this appeal for the runaway slave Paul seems unconcerned for the awful conditions in which some slaves lived. He expresses no righteous indignation over the idea of slavery and no wish to set the slave free.

Despite the obliqueness of Paul's request, we can begin to discern Paul's priorities. He is concerned in the first place for the quality of love exemplified by Philemon (the "you" in vs. 4ff. is singular), the well-being of the saints (vs. 5, 7), the free decision-making responsibility of Philemon (vs. 14,17,20,21). To a lesser extent, he is concerned for the continued utility of Onesimus (vs. 11,13,16). Paul's priorities have more to do with relationships than with the social order. He is less concerned with the formalities of slave relationships within the state than with Christian relationships within the church.

That sounds like an excuse for Paul, and in part that is true. It seems never to have occurred to Paul that slavery ought not to exist, as a matter of principle. Could he even imagine such a culture? When he says in Galatians that in Christ there is neither slave nor free, he seems to mean that the difference between them, if they are both "in Christ," does not matter.

This, then, is part of the reason for the obliqueness of his request to Philemon. He makes his point about a Christian master and a slave without anticipating a change in the economy or society because the Christian relationship is the crucial one. Other things pale into insignificance beside that.

It is also possible that a part of Paul's reserve stems from his own threatening circumstances. If he, as a prisoner in Rome awaiting trial on a capital charge, is sheltering a runaway slave, he will want to be careful not to add yet another offense. His situation may be very delicate. Anxiety about the reaction of the soldier, to whom Paul is chained as he dictates this letter, could be an important contributing factor.

The main thing is that Paul is deeply concerned for both Onesimus and Philemon. He does not care so much whether Onesimus is freed, as long as he has the freedom to return without fear as a Christian to Philemon. He does not care whether Philemon frees Onesimus, as long as he treats his runaway slave with love as a Christian and a friend of Paul's.

4. SLAVERY IN PAUL'S LETTERS

The closely related letter of Paul to the church at Colossae, probably written about the same time as his letter to Philemon, contains some vivid echoes of this same question. Since there is no specific issue at stake, the advice is generalized. It is found in a section often referred to as a catalog of household instructions (cf. Eph. 5:22ff.; I Peter 2:13ff.; Titus 2:1–10; Didache 4:9–11; etc.).

The picture developed hazily in Philemon is clearer here. Paul's social policy, though it is not expressed as a social policy, is not nearly as radical as some of his earlier programmatic statements. In Col. 3:22 to 4:1 Paul adopts the position that slaves should obey their masters in everything and masters should treat their slaves well. This contains no hint of social change, only of better conditions. The basis for the attitudes of slaves and masters is eschatological: slaves will receive their reward in heaven and masters should remember that they have a master in heaven. The promise and the implied threat act as motivations for Christian slaves and masters.

What is not apparent from English translations is that the whole passage plays off earthly masters *(kyrioi)* against Jesus as Lord *(kyrios)*. So we might paraphrase Paul's message in this way:

> Servants, obey in everything your earthly lords . . . because you fear the Lord. Whatever you do, work wholeheartedly as if for the Lord and not mere men, seeing that you will receive your reward from the Lord. You are serving the Lord Messiah. Wrongdoing will be repaid, and there are no distinctions made. Lords, treat your slaves justly and fairly, for you too have a Lord in heaven.

For Paul, the slave/master relationship was ambiguous. The slave, like the free, will receive an inheritance; the master, like the slave, has a Master. Lordship and servanthood are alike derived and transitory.

What is even more notable in this passage is the mutuality of the relationship between slave and master. Each has a responsibility to the other, though those responsibilities differ. They are bound—may we say by social contract—to each other. The transforming feature of that obligatory relationship, however, is the presence of the Lord Messiah. Relationships are altered in Christ because each relationship is under the Lordship of Christ. For this reason, Paul seems not to feel unduly uncomfortable with the continuation of slavery. There is no hint that things need to change outwardly, because slave/free relationships can be understood and redefined within the framework of the Christian community.

Interestingly, several features of this view are changed in the similar passage in Eph. 6:5–9. The most notable alterations are the following: *(a)* The play on lords and the Lord is greatly diminished. *(b)* Slaves are described now as slaves of Christ, and all will be rewarded whether slaves or free (cf.

Gal. 3:28). *(c)* Whereas in Colossians the idea of impartiality was applied to judgment on the wrongdoing of slaves, in Ephesians it is applied to masters who treat slaves badly. The logic is that the Lord is Lord of both slaves and masters and so deals with all impartially. It seems that conditions in Ephesus may have been worse than in Colossae, possibly because the slave owners were not properly alert to their obligations to their slaves. The differences were still small, and the advice much the same as in Colossians.

Note how different is the advice given in I Tim. 6:1–2 and Titus 2:9–10. In neither letter is there any reference to a mutual responsibility. Slave owners are left alone and only slaves are addressed. They are to be submissive, to give excellent service, to honor their masters, because right doctrine requires it (Titus 2:10). It is especially noteworthy that the existence of Christian slaves and masters in the same fellowship is creating tensions. Being brothers in Christ has led some slaves to become disrespectful (I Tim. 6:2); this must be replaced by better service, since the masters are believers! These letters presuppose a situation where the natural desire for freedom is asserting itself, and it calls forth advice aimed at keeping slaves in their proper place (cf. also I Peter 2: 18–25).

If now we turn back to Paul's first letter to the church at Corinth, written about seven or eight years earlier than Philemon and Colossians, we have a still more general statement of principle than the one we find in Colossians. In the midst of a long chapter devoted to male/female relationships (see Chapter III), which has as one of its central themes the mutuality of husband and wife, Paul says: "Let everyone lead the life which the Lord has assigned to him, and in which God has called him" (I Cor. 7:17, RSV). This principle is applied in the first instance to husband and wife, but Paul pauses to point out that it applies also to circumcised and

uncircumcised, and to slave and free. It can hardly be accidental that these are the same three issues selected for inclusion in Paul's pithy statement of Gal. 3:28: neither Jew nor
Greek, neither slave nor free, neither male nor female.

This principle, it should be noted carefully, is Paul's: "and
so I order in all the churches" (I Cor. 7:17). By enunciating
it a second time (7:20, "In whatever calling in which he was
called, each should remain in that") and a third time (7:24,
"in whatever state in which he was called, each should remain in that with God") he underlines its importance to him.
He presses the idea repeatedly that one need not worry over
a change in status. His view is that you can be a slave or be
free before the Lord because the slave is a freedman of the
Lord and the freeman is a slave of Christ.

We must now deal with an important sentence in I Cor.
7:21. Its meaning is uncertain. Paul begins: "Were you a slave
when called? Don't let it worry you. But, if you are able to
become free . . . ," and then the conclusion to the sentence
is ambiguous. It could be understood as "make use of the
opportunity" or, conversely, "make use of your present condition." That is, it could mean either "become free" or "stay
a slave," and it is impossible to be sure which Paul intends.
The former is the better solution grammatically, the latter is
the better solution according to sense. Other passages will not
help, since Paul never addresses exactly this question again.
It is, therefore, quite impossible to be dogmatic. If we choose
to imagine that Paul says: Don't even accept the opportunity
to be free if you are now a slave, we shall have to sharpen up
even more his conservative social policy. If we see this as
permission to become free, against the principle (repeated
three times in eight verses) not to seek to alter one's state, we
have more of an opportunity to imagine that Paul thinks of
change as unthreatening.

5. SLAVERY AS A SYMBOL

The comments on I Cor. 7:17–24 can serve as a suitable
introduction to one last feature of the slave/free contrast in
Paul's thought. As he develops his view of slavery, he does
a neat reversal on his readers by saying that slavery is freedom and freedom is slavery. It is a homiletic device, but it
is more than that. It shows how deeply rooted is Paul's
indifference to a person's condition when that person is "in
Christ." The key to this reversal is that the slave is a freedman of the Lord, and the freeman is a slave of Christ. Neither, therefore, should become a slave of men. The categories
of slave and free are not, for Paul, final or ultimate. They are
reversible, and in their reversal they can be used as pointers
to an important theological point.

Put simply, the point is that a Christian is both slave and
free. One is free in Christ, even though a slave; or a slave to
Christ, even though free. Here we have, then, the basis for
a symbolic use of "slave" to refer to the Christian's relationship to Christ.

The idea recurs later in the same letter (I Cor. 9:19–23; cf.
9:27, where he uses a verb that suggests that he enslaves his
body) where the slavery in view is Paul's own slavery as an
apostle in the service of all (see Chapter VI). A similar concern is echoed in Gal. 5:13, where the verbal form is used:
"You have been called for freedom, brothers; only don't use
that freedom as an opportunity for the flesh, but through love
serve (or be slaves to) one another." Love to one another is
the proper condition of the free man.

These two ideas are drawn loosely together in Rom. 14:18
when Paul holds that "the one who serves [is a slave to]
Christ is acceptable to God and approved by men." This
statement is found in a section of the ethical advice in that

letter which is concerned with dealing wisely and graciously with one's fellows. Don't put a stumbling block in another's way; be accommodating; don't destroy others; bear with others' weakness; and so on.

This somewhat symbolic use of slavery as a model for the Christian's relationship to Christ and to men is also founded upon the view that Christ was a slave for men. This is found dramatically embedded in a pre-Pauline hymn in Phil. 2:7. The hymn (Phil. 2:6–11) is one of the high points of the whole New Testament, yet it has not left a great mark elsewhere in Paul's theology or in other parts of the New Testament. But in this one place Paul quotes approvingly this hymn which contains the thought that Jesus took the form of a slave, humbled himself, became obedient, and died. As a result, God exalted him for his own glory. It is not farfetched to see in Paul's use of this concept part of the origin for Paul's attitude toward slavery as an adequate symbol for the Christian's relationship to God.

6. Conclusion

We have seen how reserved Paul was in dealing with the question that every slave must have asked himself: Can I not be free? Though he states at an early stage his conviction that in Christ there is neither slave nor free, in fact when he comes to work out its implications he tends to adopt a conservative attitude. Far from advising the release of slaves, he seems hardly—if at all—to envisage the possibility of their release. There is some evidence that his view became more conservative, rather than less, as time went on.

One of the results of this restrained approach was simply that the church took another eighteen hundred years to come to a clearer view. Though we may feel guilty and ashamed that this was so, it is more important to note that there was enough in Paul's letters to prod the church's conscience. He expressed some extremely important principles which could later provide a basis for a new approach.

Another result of his restraint was that he turned slave/free distinctions into a useful analogy for the Christian's service to Christ. This has continued to be a standard part of Christian vocabulary, unlike the Jew/Gentile distinction which ceased to have real force once the dimensions of the problem changed. Perhaps this symbolic use was itself one of the reasons that the slave/free question took so long to resolve. Because it was a forceful idea, when baptized into Christian terminology one did not need to take the reality itself as seriously. Service, not slavery, was the point. It could be argued that Paul's inability to solve once and for all the problem of slavery demonstrates a great weakness in his view of freedom. There is considerable truth in this. We would all feel much easier if his attitude toward freedom dealt both with circumstantial freedom and with psychological or spiritual freedom. Paul's concerns do limit his vision. Our regret that he did no more on the question of slavery—even given the social and economic realities of his day—should not blind us to his real achievement in the other areas.

Paul's catchphrase, "In Christ there is neither slave nor free," expresses only a partial truth in Paul's day. As a slogan it seemed not to catch even his own imagination except as an incentive to better Christian service.

III

Neither Male nor Female

THE THIRD of the complementary groups found in Gal. 3:28 is that of male and female. In the same way that the exclusiveness of Jews and free men is said to be broken, so Paul claims that the male in Christ no longer can exercise the same prerogatives as he formerly could claim. As with slave and free, this is an issue that Paul does not fully resolve. In fact, in discussing the male/female question he says things that actually conflict with his programmatic statement in Gal. 3:28. Does Paul really anticipate some form of sexual liberation?

As we all are too well aware, there is a prevalent and pervasive Christian attitude toward women which, for the most part, is a putdown. This is evident not only in the role that women have traditionally played in the church (and which for the most part they continue to play) but also in the attitudes toward women outside the church. To a large extent this view is supported by the interpretation of certain Biblical texts. From this base it has permeated society since the close of the New Testament.

The main offenders have been the Pauline texts. It is important, then, to reassess these in order to determine how Paul viewed the relationship between males and females in a local church setting. The applicability of Paul's view of freedom will have to be judged in part by how we assess his dealing with the male/female question. As with the question of slavery, we must be careful not to confuse twentieth-century attitudes and demands with first-century questions.

1. THE PAULINE TEXTS

The main outline of the problem can be briefly described. In Gal. 3:25ff. Paul, early in his ministry, suggests that in the time of faith the law is no longer in charge. Through faith we are all God's children in union with Christ Jesus. Therefore there is no difference between Jew and Greek, slave and free, male and female. A qualification, however, is found in I Cor. 11:2–16. There Paul argues that women should keep their heads covered in worship services because of the relationship between man and woman that goes back to creation: man reflects the image and glory of God and woman reflects the glory of man, since she was created from man (I Cor. 11:7–8). This contributes to Paul's hierarchical understanding of creation as: God—Christ—man—woman (I Cor. 11:3). It results in Paul's claim that a man must participate in worship with his head uncovered, but a woman with her head covered (I Cor. 11:4–6).

In I Cor. 14:34–35 Paul requires that women not speak in church; they should remain subordinate, as the law demands (v. 34), and depend, apparently, upon instruction at home from their husbands after the service is over (v. 35). Earlier in this same letter Paul considers several questions on which his advice has been sought (7:1–7, 10–16, 32–38). The first of these has to do with marital relationships and the changes necessary in them because of the urgency of the times and the expectation of the end (7:26,29,31,35). Paul states that, for the most part, these relationships should remain as usual. Wife and husband should continue to live together (7:2), enjoy sexual relationships (7:3–6), and not separate (7:10–11) even if one partner is an unbeliever (7:12–16).

Later, in Col. 3:18, Paul instructs wives to be subject to husbands (and husbands to love their wives), because the Lord finds that fitting. Earlier in the same chapter Paul almost repeats his Galatians' statement when he says, "Here there cannot be Greek and Jew, circumcised and uncircumcised, barbarian, Scythian, slave, freeman, but Christ is all in all." He omits completely the male/female pair and shifts the focus from a here-and-now emphasis to a future state (Col. 3:4; cf. 3:8, 11).

A parallel section in Ephesians (Eph. 5:21–33) contains an expanded piece of instruction. It argues that wives are to be subject to their husbands as to the Lord, because the husband has a relationship to his wife analogous to the church's relationship to Christ. At the same time, husbands are to love their wives, analogous to Christ's love for the church. The sum total is that a man is to love his wife and a wife is to respect her husband (v. 33).

I Timothy 2:9–15 ostensibly deals with the dress and appearance of women in churches. In addition, it is argued that women should learn in silence and should not have authority over men because Adam was created before Eve, who was the first to transgress against God.

From this résumé it is obvious that, on the one hand, Paul describes a warm, loving relationship between man and woman in marriage, the effect of which can only be to elevate the church's understanding of women. On the other hand, there is frequently a strict limiting of the role of women, particularly in the church. The tension between these two features is rather marked.

2. THE CONTEMPORARY BACKGROUND

Paul's ambivalence should be viewed in the light of his inheritance from Jesus. Though Jesus makes no pronouncements about women and their role, his practice is illuminating in several respects.

Women were more prominent in the ministry of Jesus than one would expect from the prevailing attitudes toward women among contemporary rabbis and orthodox Pharisees or Sadducees. Women follow him, they minister to his needs, they are permitted intimacy of contact, which shocks even his closest followers. They are primary witnesses to the resurrection in all the Gospels and in some of the Gospels a woman is the first to see the risen Jesus. This is true in John, in Mark's longer ending, and in Matthew. Luke holds back from stating the chronological priority of women at the resurrection, and Paul, in I Cor., ch. 15, makes no mention of women at all. Despite the later embarrassment at women's role in the resurrection, the Gospels do not hesitate to describe the openness of Jesus' contacts with them.

It is difficult to move from Jesus' practice to a firm conclusion about his attitude toward women and their role. We may circle around that question by claiming, negatively, that Jesus did not change their role in any radical way by the commissions or responsibilities he gave them. Positively we may claim that he provided a practical basis for further developments by establishing a kind of precedent. But the absence of explicit teaching on the question must caution us against claiming too much. Though he must have been somewhat different from other rabbis in this matter, he was not glaringly different.

In Acts, women play a part in breaking old patterns of prayer behavior right after the resurrection, with the women and Mary being mentioned even ahead of Jesus' brothers (Acts 1:14). They are included as heirs to the prophecy of Joel, which Peter claims was fulfilled on the Day of Pentecost, that both "menservants and maidservants" shall prophesy (Acts 2:18, quoting Joel 2:29). Luke gives some evidence of this fulfillment through his reference to Philip's daughters' prophesying (Acts 21:9). He also refers to Priscilla's help in expounding the Scriptures more accurately to Apollos (Acts 18:26). Acts also gives an important place to Tabitha, who was "full of good works and acts of charity" (Acts 9:36), whom Peter, after being besieged by the laments of the widows in the community, raised to life (Acts 9:37–42).

In each of these cases women are presented in a somewhat surprising way. None of the activities are unique in the Jewish tradition, but the combination of roles they play is quite significant. They pray alongside men, prophesy, engage in charitable acts. This general portrayal is consistent with Luke's intention to show how the new Christian community is a community of the Spirit. One way is through the new opportunities open to women.

In the Judaism of the period, women were regarded ambivalently. On the one hand, they were held in high honor and respect; on the other hand, they were considered inferior to men. There seems to be little difference between Pharisees and Sadducees on this question. Among the Essene group at Qumran celibacy was the ideal and women were given a status even more inferior than was usual in Judaism. A later statement of the Talmud is characteristic: "Happy is he whose children are males, and woe to him whose children are females" (b.Kiddushim 82b). To have many male children was a blessing; females were not only less desirable, they were the source of many of the evils of this life. In the synagogue women were separated off behind a screen, being allowed no function in the service. Indeed the law was not applicable to women in the same way as to men: "The man who teaches his daughter the *torah* teaches her extravagance" (j.Sota 3:4). She did not have the same responsibility to keep the *torah,* and she was not to witness, instruct children, or pray at the table. At the same time, it is only fair to point out that in spite of this attitude, women sometimes played decisive roles in Jewish affairs. Alexandra (76–67 B.C.) was allowed to rule on her own after the death of her two husbands, who were brothers and both of whom were kings. The story of Judith indicates the high esteem in which women might be held.

In the Old Testament, Miriam (Ex. 15:20), Deborah (Judg. 4:4ff.; 5:1ff.), Huldah (II Kings 22:14), and Esther all have significant "official" functions. In addition, we should note the inclusion of The Book of Ruth in the Hebrew Scriptures. These provide some relief from the theoretical attitude toward men's superiority.

A woman's role as wife and mother is strongly reinforced in the Old Testament, and this positive assessment of her place is augmented by the personal and cultic rights that she enjoyed. At the same time, it is assumed either explicitly or implicitly that she should not aspire to a larger role. The whole cultural and social fabric of Judaism presupposes a greatly restricted sphere of activity, based upon an assumption that woman was legally more a chattel than a person in Israel.

In the Oriental world the social and cultural situation was not so very different. As one moves westward in the ancient world, one finds that greater freedom was often accorded women. Thus, in the Doric world, and in Rome, women had many of the privileges and freedoms that men enjoyed. The Greek and the Roman ideal was a relatively lofty one, though in practice women were not treated with the same respect and honor that characterized Jewish attitudes toward women. In the area of sexual relationships, Greek and Roman women assumed a freedom unknown in Judaism. While marriage, and even monogamy, was the general rule, freer sexual relationships often modified the ideal, and in the period of the early church the incidence of divorce was increasing rather rapidly.

3. WOMEN IN THE CORINTHIAN CHURCH

It is not always recognized that there was a dispute in the congregation in Corinth precisely because women were taking part in the services of worship. The dispute was probably based upon different attitudes toward the validity of this participation and different arguments about the need to follow the practice of the synagogue. In I Cor., ch. 11, Paul acknowledges that women are praying and prophesying in public worship (11:5). He does not suggest that they should cease. Instead, he commends the congregation in 11:2 because it follows the tradition he handed on to them (cf. also 11:23) and thereby may imply that the practice of women praying and prophesying in the community gatherings is something he taught them. Even if this is not a correct inference, the practice did spring up. Whatever its visible origin, it was a result of a newfound freedom in the Spirit.

Paul demanded only that women keep their heads covered, because he believed that a hierarchy existed in the form of: God—Christ—man—woman. He based his view on creation and the Fall (11:7ff.). In the contemporary Jewish world, and in the preceding century or so, there had been a considerable increase in speculation about the effects of the Fall, and the first man, Adam. This speculation was the background against which Paul's view of Christ as the last Adam and Christians as the New Creation must be viewed. It is also the conceptual background for his interpretation of Scripture. His argument is inferential, based upon his perception of the logic inherent in the order of priority at creation and apparently upon Gen. 3:16: "He shall be your master."

It was generally held that women had a secondary role because of the derivative creation of woman in the creation story in Gen., ch. 2, and because woman is more susceptible to temptation and therefore to sin (Gen., ch. 3). A legend exists, about the time of the New Testament, that Eve was seduced sexually by the serpent; this would help to account for the inferiority ascribed to her (e.g., Genesis Rabbah 18; IV Macc. 18:7–8). Though that is obviously legendary, it is possible that, in Gen. 3:16, the word "rule" should be interpreted in a sexual sense, i.e., that the woman is for the sexual service of man. It is apparent that the rest of the report of God's words to Eve deals with childbearing and her desire for her husband. The usual Hebrew parallelism in the first two lines,

> I will greatly multiply your pain in childbearing;
> in pain you shall bring forth children,

should perhaps be complemented with

> yet your desire will be for your husband,
> and he shall fulfill his desire upon you.

If this were so, most of the arguments for male superiority drawn from the Fall narratives would fall. Though this might be a more adequate interpretation of Gen., chs. 2 to 3, in our day, it is not the way in which the passage was interpreted by Paul.

When Paul quotes Gen. 1:27 (I Cor. 11:7ff.) he develops a rabbinic tradition (see Numbers Rabbah 3:8 and Rashi on Isa. 44:13). He does not make a fresh assessment of the significance of the verse and consequently he does not give due weight to the idea that human likeness to God at creation extends to both male and female. The Hebrew *adam* is used generically for "humans" in Gen. 1:26–27; hence when the author wished to distinguish, he used the particular words "male" *(zakar)* and "female" *(negebah)*. This inclusion of both male and female in the term *adam* is evident also from the phrase in Gen. 1:26: "Let *them* have dominion." Some contemporary Jewish documents express the idea that Adam, at creation, was bisexual (e.g., Genesis Rabbah 8:1; and in Babylonian Talmud Erubin 18a; Berakoth 61a).

However, in the other account of creation (Gen. 2:4ff.), where man is placed at the head of creation (2:7), there is a much greater disjunction between the creation of man and woman In Gen., ch. 2, *adam* is used both of man as opposed to woman and also generically (as in Gen., ch. 1) but without the same sense of inclusion of the female. Thus, when woman is created, the writer in ch. 2 does not use the word for "female" but a word for woman derived from another of the words for man—*ishshah* (2:22). Contemporary Jews recognized the difficulty inherent in the two creation accounts. Philo, for example, who died in about A.D. 54, speculated that Gen., ch. 1, described the creation of ideal man (the Logos) and Gen., ch. 2, described the creation of the man Adam. While Paul does not follow that lead, he does appear to prefer the second account of creation, which comes from a different source.

But Paul's main concern in I Cor., ch. 11, is with the practice of head covering. The important issue is that hair serves as a covering for a woman's head in a way not true for man. Hair distinguishes between man and woman, and is a symbol for that difference. Apparently Paul's view of this matter was deeply affected by inherited attitudes, and was not really based upon his understanding of Scripture. The traditional Jewish practice was for men to have short hair, for women to have long hair and to keep their heads covered. The covering is a symbol of subjection to the male, and a sign of respect for the divine order. The angels, who according to rabbinic speculation were active at creation, require this sign of "authority" to be placed on women's heads. Paul here follows this form of argumentation without the Scriptural base for it that appears necessary. He reinforces his justification for the restriction by referring to "nature" (I Cor. 11: 13–15).

There are several indications in this section of breaks in logic. For example, there is no reason why an unveiled head for a woman is as shameful as if her head were shaved; nor is there any obvious reason for it being shameful if a man prays with his head covered (11:4–9). Indeed, the practice in modern Judaism is the reverse of the practice in Paul's day: men pray with heads covered. Paul argues the point a second time, basing his view on angels (11:10), and then attempts a third form of argument (11:13–15), which deals with the length of hair. But if long hair can be considered as covering the head when it is a question of men's practice, why can it not be considered to cover the head when women are praying (11:15b; cf. 11:4–5)? In the argument we see evidence of Paul's discomfiture, which results in the rather petulant conclusion: "But if anyone wants to argue about it, all I have to say is that neither we nor the churches of God have any other habit in worship" (11:16).

To recapitulate, Paul's argument depends upon four basic assertions: (1) There is a hierarchical order in which woman is last. (2) Man's head ought not to be covered because of his place in the hierarchy. (3) Woman's hair is an indication of pride and therefore the head needs to be covered before God. (4) The angels demand a covering for women. None of these assertions, so far as I can trace, is explicitly Scriptural. Nor is the connection between them logical. The argument resembles a *haggadic* presentation of a rabbi without the *midrashic* exposition on which the *haggadah* is based.

In this passage, let us remind ourselves, women are still allowed to pray and prophesy. Paul can also state unequivocally that "in the Lord woman is not independent of man nor man of woman; for as woman was made from man, so man is now born of woman" (11:11–12). Man and woman complement each other. This is a new idea and specific to Christianity. This new statement gets buried underneath the logic of Paul's other arguments.

Paul's comments in I Cor., ch. 11, raise two separate questions: the relationship of male and female and the role of women in worship. These are each expanded elsewhere in the letter, the former in I Cor., ch. 7, and the latter in I Cor., ch. 14. We shall pursue the latter first.

When Paul considers public worship, in I Cor. 14:34–35 (a passage sometimes viewed as a non-Pauline interpolation), he deals with the question of women speaking in church meetings. Either they are asking their husbands or one of the speakers about the significance of something during the service, or they wish to contribute to the meeting, or perhaps both. Paul demands a change in this practice. He justifies his request by referring to some Jewish law about the subordination of women. This law is not specified but is probably Gen. 3:16. We may infer that the screen separating women from men has been broken down. Not all synagogue practices still obtain. As we saw from I Cor., ch. 11, women are allowed to take part in the worship service. Then why the curious distinction: implicit permission to pray and prophesy but refusal to allow speaking?

The situation must be understood as evidence for Paul's ambivalence about the desirable degree of innovation in church worship. He is of two minds, but not to such an extent that he tackles the issues head on. Women in the church at Corinth are becoming emancipated by comparison with women in the synagogue. They may sit with their husbands (but must not create a disturbance) and they may pray and prophesy (charismatic activities that must not be quenched, see Chapter VII). The change in attitude both toward female participation and toward the physical arrangements in the small church can only be seen as a major change in the inherited Jewish practice.

In order not to sever all relationships with the Jewish community, Paul advises some concessions, mostly at the level of practices inherited from the oral tradition of Judaism. He wishes to keep himself and the Corinthians sufficiently within Jewish norms to maintain a distinction from the prevailing Greco-Roman behavior. Confusion with Hellenism might occur if women no longer respected the primacy of their husbands. It would not do for a Christian woman to be mistaken for a heathen woman, nor to assert such a degree of freedom that she would be confused with the prostitutes, whether cultic or commercial, who were rather common in Corinth. Too much sexual freedom would create problems for the church's mission to Jews and associate it with the Hellenistic mystery religions.

In these two passages Paul gives indirect evidence of a considerable freeing of the attitudes toward women. But he fights on two fronts. On the one front he is conscious of the pressures to conform to Jewish attitudes and practices. On the other he is sensitive to the danger of confusion between Christian women and unredeemed Greek women because of the scorn and damage that might follow if such confusion arose. As will appear from the next two chapters, it is likely that these two fronts can be related to fractures within the Corinthian congregation.

Paul's treatment of the relationship between male and female is much simpler. The theme of I Cor., ch. 7, is mutuality, a notion that is also hinted at in I Cor. 11:11 and will be developed later in Colossians and Ephesians. In this chapter virtually everything said about man is also said about woman. Thus a man should have his own wife, a woman her own husband (7:2); the husband should give to his wife her conjugal rights, and the wife to the husband (7:3); the husband rules the wife's body and the wife her husband's (7:4); neither is to refuse the other (7:5); the wife should not separate from the husband, the husband should not divorce his wife (7:10–11); the believing husband should not divorce an unbelieving wife, and vice versa (7:12–13). As the chapter unfolds, this sense of complete equality within the husband/wife relationship is confirmed (e.g., 7:32–34).

Paul goes further in I Cor., ch. 7, than in any of his other statements. In such a passage it would have been easy to include comments about male superiority. He does not. Its phrasing must be intentional. To omit any notion of the husband's authority likewise appears intentional. As it stands, the statement is so strong an assertion of mutual trust, responsibility, and service that it must have been an almost shockingly novel notion in the prevailing culture. This novelty even includes important changes in the manner in which Jewish marriages could be terminated.

The chapter also includes, in 7:17–24, consideration of two other matters. Paul deals with slave/free in 7:21–24 (see Chapter II) and with the circumcised/uncircumcised in 7:17–20 (see Chapter I). The three issues are the same three found in Gal. 3:28, and are also linked in Colossians and Ephesians.

In the cases of both slave/free and circumcised/uncircumcised one is not to seek to change his status. Paul is concerned —perhaps overly concerned—for the social fabric. He does not urge solutions that will upset the social order unduly. But he does urge solutions that radically call into question inherited notions of private or public morality and the relationships between people. In each case, then, Paul is stating an ideal that is to be implemented in Christian relationships. In the case of husbands and wives it is a remarkable statement devoid of any assertion of male dominance.

When Paul urges male priority, as he does in I Cor., chs. 11 and 14, it is because of the social and ecclesiastical situation confronting him. His failure to carry through his generous attitude toward females—expressed in I Cor., ch. 7—should not blind us to the importance of that chapter in any reconstruction of Paul's views.

4. LATER PAULINE ATTITUDES

The statement in Gal. 3:28 is Paul's boldest assertion of the breaking down of three walls: "In Christ there is neither Jew nor Gentile, slave nor free, male nor female." It can hardly be accidental that it includes a summary statement of exactly the same three issues that were dealt with in I Cor., ch. 7. The programmatic assertion of Galatians has been worked out in greater detail in that chapter, especially with regard to male and female. It is striking that two of the three are alluded to in Col. 3:11, the third one following later in v. 18. In Eph., chs. 5 to 6, two of the matters are referred to side by side (Eph. 5:21–33 and 6:5–9), while the third is referred to much earlier in the letter (Eph. 2:11–22).

These passages in Colossians and Ephesians indicate a withdrawal from Paul's previous statements in I Corinthians in at least two respects: first, while he still asserts the mutuality of the relationship between male and female, he qualifies it with an emphasis on the husband's authority; second, while he still asserts the restrictions on the role of women in church, he does not acknowledge that women are playing some part in public worship.

When, in Col. 3:11, Paul parallels the statement made in

Gal. 3:28, he includes the Jew/Greek and the slave/free disjunctions, but he leaves out the male/female one. It is difficult to see why this should be, unless he finds it an embarrassment. It is all the more curious that, as he proceeds into the section of advice, he does deal with the relationship between males and females within marriage. The paragraph Col. 3:18 to 4:1 contains an expression of the need for mutuality between husband/wife, child/parent, slave/master. These relationships are interdependent because the people so related are all "in Christ." There can be no Jew or Greek, slave or free, etc. This is "the new nature which is being renewed in knowledge after the image of its creator" (Col. 3:10). Part of that new creation is the establishing of a relationship between wives and husbands which "images" the creator.

However, within that relationship Paul is quite adamant in his view of authority: "Wives, be subject to your husbands, as is fitting in the Lord" (Col. 3:18). The sentence is balanced by a reference to husbands' love for their wives, and is complemented by statements about the obedience of children and the fairness of fathers, the obedience of slaves and the fairness of masters. While this stress on the husband's authority is consistent with the *assumption* that lies behind I Cor., ch. 11 (and perhaps I Cor., ch. 14), it is noteworthy that it is being expressed for the first time here, toward the end of Paul's ministry.

Ephesians is often rejected as not being a genuine Pauline letter, and there are good reasons for the skepticism. But for our purposes, we may consider it as being genuinely from Paul. The section that deals with husbands and wives is a part of the instructional section of the letter beginning with Eph. 4:1. Standing over all this is the notion that Christians are to "forbear one another in love" (4:2). This leads to a stress on the unity of the Spirit, the one body, and complementarity of the gifts within that body, etc. The same idea is picked up in 5:21 in the general statement introducing the section: "Be subject to one another out of reverence for Christ." As in Colossians, that section deals with husbands/wives, children/parents, slaves/masters, in the same order. These important social stratifications are to be dealt with by as much mutual subjection as possible. Slaves are to obey their masters; children are to obey their parents. But masters are "subject" to slaves in the sense of being just and nonthreatening; parents are "subject" to children by not provoking them. So also with respect to the husband/wife relationship: wives are to be subject to husbands, as to the Lord; husbands are to love their wives, as Christ loves the church. The fuller development of these positions stresses the analogies to Christ and the church. There is again a mutuality which is very attractive.

When Paul goes on to quote Gen. 2:24, that man shall be joined to his wife and the two shall become one (Eph. 5:31), he underlines the mystery of the text and its applicability to Christ and the church (5:32), though, as the next verse indicates, he has not lost sight of his original intention and refers it also to husband and wife (5:33). Paul is developing his Adam concern (cf. also Rom., ch. 5, and I Cor., ch. 15) as applied to husband/wife relationships. He sees creation returning to a new creation where male and female are restored to a primal type of marital relationship. There are still differences—a husband "loves" his wife, a wife "respects" her husband, but each is subject to the other, because they have become "one."

A consistent picture emerges from Colossians and Ephesians, a picture of a daring thinker becoming more restrained as time goes on. The ideas are much the same, but the stress is different. The radical implications for the social fabric of some of his earlier statements are now sidestepped by a fresh attention to matters of social order: obedience, respect, honor (e.g., Eph. 5:22,24,33; 6:1,2,5).

5. I Timothy, ch. 2

The passage in I Timothy has additional complications, the most obvious of which is the prevalent questioning of Pauline authorship. There are substantial difficulties connected with the ascription of the letter to Paul. One possibility is that it originates with Paul, but comes actually from the pen of Luke, who writes at Paul's direction, though not by dictation, while Paul is in prison at Rome. If so, what we have is partly Lukan and partly Pauline theology. Luke is given instructions to write on certain subjects to Timothy; he takes what he knows Paul to have said earlier on the subject and develops it in his own fashion.

In I Tim., ch. 2, the same kind of argument is made as in I Cor., chs. 11 and 14, except that it is extended to prohibit women from teaching and having authority over men. The relationship between Adam and Eve is developed and explicitly related to women in church. The argument, curiously, is more typically rabbinic than in I Corinthians. It preserves (by a summarizing allusion, not by quotation) the Scriptural basis on which the writer makes his assertions that Adam has chronological priority over Eve and that Eve is the first transgressor. The exegetical steps are clearer in this instance, and so are the results: the sole right of men to teach in worship. This result overlooks the fact that, logically, no necessary inference need be drawn from Adam's chronological priority or from Eve's transgression. Perhaps that contributes to the abruptness. There is no appeal to tradition or custom; Pauline authority is sufficient (I Tim. 2:12).

One of the perplexities of this passage is the appended

conclusion. How woman will be saved through childbearing
is not clear and has been hotly debated. It may, in some
obscure way, refer to Gen. 3:16, the very passage that is used
to demonstrate male superiority. If so, we have a complex
exegesis of the creation accounts in which two quite different
conclusions emerge: one deals with man's superiority, the
other with woman's special place in God's scheme for salvation because of her role in the Fall.

The first part of this passage in I Tim., ch. 2, is more
confusing. Verse 8 deals with men taking part in the service,
specifically praying, and vs. 11–14 deal with women in public
worship. But vs. 9–10 deal with women's apparel. Why this
break in subject matter? The answer emerges out of the gram-
mar of the sentence. In v. 9 there is no verb, as often happens
in Greek. In supplying a verb, most translations use a form
of the verb "to be." This may be incorrect. The sentence
begins, "Likewise also women," referring back in a parallel
structure to "I desire that men pray." The parallel is quite
precise; one would expect, on the basis of the location of the
verb "to pray" in v. 8, that the strong connective "likewise"
implies the inclusion of "to pray" in the next sentence. If we
should supply for the verb that is missing "to pray" instead
of "to be," the verse should be translated: "Likewise also
women (when they pray) should be modest, sensible," etc.
The point that the author is making is that when women
participate in public worship they should not draw attention
to themselves by their appearance. They are to be bearers of
the message from God or to God in prayer without ostenta-
tion.

We find in I Timothy a more developed situation, but still
quite similar to that obtaining in I Corinthians. Women may
pray; they may not speak or exercise authority. The Biblical
basis for this view is somewhat more clearly stated than in
I Corinthians, though the actual situation in the church ad-

dressed does not show through as well. The teaching in I Tim. 2:12 is not so smothered with qualifications; the question about women's authority over men is raised directly and then rejected.

6. CONCLUSION

In his own lifetime Paul worked through to a genuine solution to the Jew/Gentile problem. Because it was so crucial to the life of the church, he concentrated upon it. He did not really resolve the slave/free problem, because he was not as deeply implicated in that issue. But he did set out a concern for the slave/free relationship in Colossians, Philemon, and Ephesians which bore fruit eighteen hundred years later. His own reserve in the face of an acute social problem made him counsel a radical shift in the attitude of Christians toward slaves and of Christian slaves toward their masters, but not a freeing of slaves.

Paul did not resolve the male/female problem, though he went further in establishing a solution than we usually recognize. Not only did the churches he founded break the usual pattern of Jewish restrictiveness toward women, he also broke at one level the theoretical subjugation of women. His statement in Gal. 3:28 is an exact reversal of a synagogue prayer: "Lord, I thank you that you did not create me a barbarian (Greek), a slave, or a woman." Only men could pray that prayer, and indeed they were to pray it three times a day. But Paul's cry could be echoed by all Christians as a claim to a new kind of social order that might begin in the church. The tragedy is that it seems to have died before it began.

The importance of Gal. 3:28 is that, without any qualifications or reservations, Paul states explicitly (perhaps even naively) the possibility of new relationships. In the same way

that the circumcised have no exclusive priority over the uncircumcised and the free have no exclusive advantage over
the slave, so Paul says the male has no advantage over the
female. Yet at the same time he develops a notion of male
authority.

Paul lived in the real world. As he gave pastoral advice to
congregations, he often found it necessary to advise something less than his own best insights. Sometimes those insights were modified by deeply buried personal reservations.
In the case of women he insists upon a reserved emancipation, allowing participation in some parts of church activity,
such as praying and prophesying, but holding back in other
areas. The reasons for this ambivalence may be a combination of factors: his concern that there not be confusion among
the Greeks that Christianity was antithetical to Judaism; and
a personal set of convictions inherited from his past, the
extent of which we cannot now establish. Sexual liberation
was not carried out by Paul, but it had begun.

The following points may act as a summary:

a. Pauline churches allowed women to pray and prophesy
in public worship and to engage in some other important
leadership activities.

b. Paul himself, either for short-term reasons or because
of deep-seated convictions inherited from Judaism, did not
argue with his churches for the full emancipation of women
in worship.

c. Paul's view was apparently based upon Gen., chs. 1 to
3, utilizing certain rabbinic methods of inference and exegesis, though we have no single example in which Paul develops
as thoroughly as we should like his method for coming to his
conclusions. In some cases his views are presented as traditional customs which require assent.

d. There were pressures on Paul to restrict the role of
women. From the Jewish side, inherited custom was ex-

tremely important for all who, like Paul, valued their Judaism and the revelation of God to Israel. From the pagan side the danger of confusion with pagan life and mystery religions suggested a cautious policy. There may also have been a radical party arguing for full emancipation right away, which would have led to a "go slow and avoid confusion" policy.

e. Paul's boldest insight comes earliest: "In Christ there is neither male nor female." He pursues this in the case of marriage in I Cor., ch. 7, but holds back from it in the church situation in I Cor., chs. 11, 14, and elsewhere.

f. Paul argued both for and against a husband's authority in marriage. The argument for is explicit; the argument against is implicit. The question of the male role in the church is, for Paul, the trickiest question. Even though he describes an ideal view of the marital relationship in I Cor., ch. 7, he still seems tied to an assumption of male dominance. Even though he allowed female participation in worship, he still holds back from full participation. It is probably not accidental that the strongest assertions of male dominance in marriage come in Colossians and Ephesians, the most heavily ecclesiastical letters.

g. There is some evidence that Paul views renewed male/female relationships "in Christ" as an indispensable part of the new creation, contingent upon the death and resurrection of Jesus, the new, second, or last Adam. If this is the case, he is proposing a reversal of the results of the Fall which ought to include (and perhaps does in Gal. 3:28 and I Cor., ch. 7) a reversal of the mastery of man over woman.

h. More speculative is the possibility that in establishing his new creation motif Paul is attempting also to move back even behind Gen., ch. 2 (on which he bases his convictions about male authority in the church) to a renewed understanding of the unity of mankind—male and female—presented in Gen. 1:26–27. It seems to be the case that Paul's view of the Body of Christ is based at least partly on this creation motif of unity. If so, there is no *a priori* reason against unity of male and female, as hinted in Gal. 3:28. Christ, as the last Adam, is the progenitor of the church, his body which reduplicates the creation of *adam* in Gen. 1: 26–27.

Western civilization has been moving toward a more liberated view of women and of male/female relationships in the last hundred years. The church, however, is still a place where women play subordinate roles, and this subordination is founded upon Paul's statement. However, there is some reason for urging that Paul's view be interpreted more liberally than it often is. If so, the church's reconsideration of the role of women must be accelerated and women accorded a place more nearly like the place they occupied in Corinth.

IV

Firmness and Flexibility

PAUL'S CHURCHES were made up of varying mixtures of Jewish and Gentile Christians. This variety inevitably gave rise to problems within these churches. There were varying degrees of conservatism and liberalism, mostly with respect to the need for following Jewish law and customs. On specific moral and practical questions different answers could be given, and these differences would increase with their degree of "indifference." Sabbath observance raised more problems than sexual ethics, and eating practices more than both (see Rom. 14:1–9; Col. 3:16–19). On questions that were fundamental to faith in Jesus—messiahship, redemption, sin, future hope—there was likely to be less occasion for confrontation in the churches.

Paul's understanding of what a Christian is encouraged him to adopt a view that Spirit, not law, directs the Christian life. This was such a fundamental point for Paul that he must have found it difficult to "lay down the law" when faced with differences of opinion. We need first of all to look at how he gave specific commands and advice, and then to look at his more general principle "to be all things to all men" and determine how that principle was to be applied.

1. PAUL AND OBEDIENCE

Most of Paul's advice is found in the paraenetic section of his letters—that is, the section giving ethical advice and exhortation.

This advice section is seen most easily in Philemon, Paul's shortest and simplest letter. Having stated that he expects Philemon to receive Onesimus back with open arms, he closes the body of the letter in v. 20. In v. 21 the paraenetic section opens with "Confident of your obedience. . . ." As well as stipulating that he expects Philemon's concurrence, he also asks that a room be prepared for him. Here, then, Paul deals not with theoretical questions but with live issues that require action. Even though he wishes Philemon's consent to be free, not forced (v. 14), he still asks for obedience. A fine line is drawn between forced behavior and voluntary agreement (see vs. 8–9).

In Galatians the paraenetic section begins in 5:1 with the statement "For freedom Christ sets us free," to which is appended a whole series of advisory and hortatory statements. In Gal. 5:2–12, Paul continues his view of the need for freedom in the Spirit; in 5:13–15 he qualifies that freedom with the need for love; in 5:16–24 he lists the results of following flesh and of following the Spirit, where he repeats that the law cannot create such fruit (v. 23). He then urges that they bear each other's burdens (6:1–6), using an unusual phrase, "the law of Christ," in 6:2, and closes this section of the letter with advice on doing good to all (6:7–10). With this we begin to sense something of the tension between law and Spirit, between command and inward motivation.

The Thessalonian correspondence shows even more clearly the kind of exhortations Paul gave. In I Thess. 4:1, the beginning of the paraenetic section, Paul "beseeches and ex-

horts" them to please God: the way to do so is to follow
Paul's teaching. The advice is "to do so more and more" (I
Thess. 4:2,10). Paul has taught them (I Thess. 4:1), the Holy
Spirit teaches them (I Thess. 4:8), God has taught them (I
Thess. 4:9). Paul does not hesitate to say what he takes to be
the will of God (I Thess. 5:18), yet he immediately balances
this by stating that they must not quench the Spirit (I Thess.
5:19) or despise prophesying (I Thess. 5:20). Something of
the same impression is conveyed in II Thessalonians when
Paul interjects an expression of his confidence that they will
do the things he commands (II Thess. 3:4) between a statement that the Lord will strengthen them (II Thess. 3:3) and
a wish that the Lord may direct them to the love of God and
the obedience of Christ (II Thess. 3:5). But having said that,
he then issues commands (II Thess. 3:6,12; cf. 3:10), and
confirms this even more strongly in v. 14 when he threatens
any who refuse to obey.

In Romans the paraenetic section begins with Rom. 12:1:
"I appeal to you therefore . . . ." This especially gentle and
lengthy passage covering most of Rom., chs. 12 to 15, is
addressed to a congregation he apparently does not know.
His mild instruction never goes beyond advice and exhortation. The form "let us" is used in most of what he says here.

The Philippian letter is addressed to the congregation with
whom Paul's relationships were friendliest. As in Romans,
the advice is good-natured. It begins in Phil. 2:12 on the note
of obedience, though there is no specific demand requiring
obedience. Even when dealing with the pressing question of
disagreement between Euodia and Syntyche, Paul only "ex-
horts," he does not command (Phil. 4:2–3).

In Colossians, though the advice with respect to slaves and
women is more conservative (see Chapters II and III), there
is no command in the paraenetic section.

In brief, in Paul's correspondence apart from I Corinthians

we find a constantly shifting balance between the demands he lays on his congregations and the advice he offers them. As one who is an apostle and therefore, presumably, more mature, he sometimes feels free to demand obedience, and at other times he holds back. In the letters to the Romans and the Colossians—congregations that he has not founded—he simply offers advice. In some cases he explicitly draws attention to the real source of obedience and ethical behavior found in the relationship with God and the motivating power of the Holy Spirit. But on occasion he requires that congregations he has founded follow his orders. This does not happen frequently, but often enough that we must allow for some notion of apostolic authority imposed at least on that limited number of congregations which owe their origin to him.

It is essential to note that primitive Christian communities did not adopt a laissez-faire attitude toward ethics. Behavior was extremely important. Improper behavior was condemned and good behavior praised. It was not enough for Paul simply to leave them on their own with the Holy Spirit. Important as the Spirit was in directing the morality and conduct of Christians, advice, exhortation, and encouragement from those more mature was still necessary because of the struggle between flesh and Spirit, between law and license. Consistently maturing behavior was most important. Basically the goal was to be an imitator of Paul, an imitator of Christ, filled with the fruit of the Spirit.

2. A PRINCIPLE OF ADAPTABILITY

In I Corinthians, to which we now turn, the question of Christian behavior is crucial. Most of the letter contains advice from Paul to the church at Corinth, a good bit of it occasioned by requests from the Corinthians for his opinion.

The advice itself begins in ch. 5 and runs through to ch. 16. The questions asked by the Corinthians are introduced in 7:1 ("Now concerning the things about which you wrote . . ."). The subjects deal with marriage (7:1ff.), the unmarried (7:25ff.), food offered to idols (8:1ff.), spiritual gifts (12:1ff.), and Paul's offering for Jerusalem (16:1ff.). It is not clear whether the discussion of the resurrection originates in a question by the Corinthians.

The study of I Corinthians should form the center of any assessment of Paul's view of Christian ethics for several reasons: *(a)* It includes the fullest treatment of a wide range of problems. *(b)* It is in response to questions from the church itself, and therefore deals with mutually recognized problems. *(c)* In it Paul is implicitly under attack and so he answers, for the most part, in careful terms. *(d)* It is addressed to a congregation about whose situation we know a fair amount. And *(e)* it states some principles of behavior not enunciated elsewhere.

One of Paul's important statements of principle, found in 10:31 to 11:1, urges the Corinthians:

> Whether you eat or drink or whatever you do, do everything for God's glory. Be blameless both to Jews and to Greeks, and to the church of God, as I also try to please everyone in everything, not seeking my own good but that of many, in order that they may be saved. Become imitators of me, as I also am of Christ.

The goal "to please everyone in everything" is expressed as a principle of *Paul's:* "I try to please everyone in everything." But it is one that the Corinthians should imitate. Although this idea occupies an important place in I Corinthians, it is not found elsewhere in Paul's correspondence. The nearest that one can come is in Rom. 14:13, where Paul suggests that no one should put a stumbling block in another's way, and in Rom. 15:2, where he advises that each is to please his neighbor for his good.

The principle expressed so forcefully in I Cor. 10:31 to 11:1 is in the context of a discussion of freedom. The beginning of the previous paragraph (10:23) expresses one of the watchwords of the Corinthian church, or of a faction within the church: "All things are lawful." Paul replies, "Yes, but not everything is helpful." The matters under dispute, and here being summed up, obviously go to the heart of the question of freedom—at least freedom as it is understood in the Corinthian church. Many of these questions derive from the differing backgrounds of those who make up the congregation, and their differing assumptions about how to deal with such questions.

In briefest terms, one part of the church—the left, if we may call it that—is constituted by spiritual enthusiasts who appear to be urging a radical view of Christianity and the effects of the Spirit in the believers' lives. Another side—we might call it the right—is constituted by the timid persons who resist innovation and want to continue to be associated closely with Jewish (or Jewish Christian) attitudes. We must not imagine too much polarization, of course. The majority probably do not fall on one side or the other but are trying to muddle through somewhere in the middle. It may be representatives of the "middle" who have written to Paul asking for advice.

Many of these questions will be discussed in the next chapter, for most are a challenge to Paul from the left. These issues he deals with, granting the correctness of certain of their basic assumptions, but taking exception to the undisciplined way in which those assumptions have been applied to concrete problems. There is another set of questions animating Paul's discussion which come from the right. These issues are less clear but appear to revolve around Paul's claim to apostleship, and specifically questions about his *own* ethical stance as an apostle. The left-wing questions are mostly about others, the right-wing ones mostly about himself. To both sets of questions Paul offers the same general conclusion: "Be blameless before everyone . . . try to please everyone, just as I do." That conclusion ties together his concern for his congregation's behavior and his anxiety over the way his own behavior is being criticized. He urges on them all the same attitude he has adopted himself toward ethical questions—though perhaps with some reservations.

3. I CORINTHIANS, CH. 9: AM I NOT FREE?

In the Corinthian correspondence, defense of Paul's apostleship is never far below the surface. In the midst of a discussion of other ethical questions, I Cor., ch. 9, brings to the surface this apologetic motif. At the same time, the chapter contains the most deliberate expression of Paul's own principle of freedom as well as the theoretical basis for what he says in summary in I Cor. 10:31 to 11:1.

Questions have been raised in Corinth about his use of Christian freedom (9:1). Though the left wing (see Chapter V) may have accused him of being too bound, the right wing thinks he is altogether too free in his behavior (9:3–12). Against the latter view Paul describes his practice and his principles. He distinguishes himself from conservatives who would ring him round with too may restrictions—restrictions that would limit his freedom in Christ. It is this that motivates him in this section of the letter.

His first line of defense of his apostleship is that he has seen Jesus the Lord (i.e., the risen Jesus). His second line is that the Corinthians, of all people, know he is an apostle because he has formed them as Christians (9:1–2; cf. II Cor. 3:1ff.; 11:2). In this same vein he continues to develop his defense by focusing on his actions. Like the other apostles, Paul and Barnabas also have the right to be accompanied by a wife (9:5). Like these others too, they have the right to claim material benefits on account of their ministry (9:3–14, especially vs. 5,6,12,14). As is well known, Paul practiced his tentmaking trade to support himself (except for gifts from the Philippian church which he accepted, see Phil. 4:10, 14ff.). He has voluntarily renounced these rights (9:12,15,18), even though the legitimate exercise of Christian freedom allows them.

He admits that his reason is that he wishes to be able to boast that the good news he preaches is free of charge (9:15–18). Simply to preach the gospel is not enough (this may be a polemic against the other apostles who *do* accept material benefits). Anyone who knows it *must* preach it. It is only a truly apostolic labor if one gives up one's rights voluntarily so that the good news comes at no material cost.

This defense is now capped by an impressive statement of neatly balanced clauses. Here he sets out in a remarkably transparent way the approach he follows in his apostolic labors. It sounds so accommodating as to be unprincipled; in fact, that is almost the case.

v. 19 For being free from all,
to all I enslaved myself,   so that I might gain the
                                       more;

v. 20 I became to Jews as a
Jew,   so that I might gain Jews;

to those under law as one
under law (not being myself
under law),   so that I might gain those
                                       under law;

v. 21 to those without law as one without law (not being without the law of God but within the law of Christ),

so that I might gain the lawless;

v. 22 I became weak to the weak,

so that I might gain the weak

to everyone I have become everything,

so that I might by all means save some;

v. 23 I do everything for the sake of the good news,

so that I might become its participant.

Paul's behavior is rescued from being unprincipled by one thing alone: his goal. The passage's pressing repetition of the phrase "so that I might gain" (five times) with the conclusion "so that I might by all means save some" is striking. His goal is the successful prosecution of the apostolic task he has been given by the risen Jesus—to gain Jews and Greeks for the good news. Only if he does this can he himself be a participant in the good news.

Paul's principle then is to accommodate himself to any condition of men if that will assist in their reception of the good news. He is at the very least willing to adapt his behavior to Jews, to those under the law, to those without the law, and to the weak. These particular categories are probably selected because of their relevance to the Corinthian church. He does not appear to give a definitive statement of the possible limits of adaptability, nor has he selected a particularly congruent set of labels. Indeed, there is no general agreement whether Paul is referring to two, three, or four kinds of persons. Regardless of that, the point is that he is willing to be flexible in certain circumstances.

These clauses are bracketed by the general conclusion, "I have become all things to all men," a statement of Paul's which is well known but generally disapproved, and the introduction which asserts his freedom from all but enslavement to all. In both the introduction and the conclusion the specific adaptations of the middle section are generalized, and attention is directed toward the bearer of the message: he enslaves himself to all even though he is supremely free; he is a participant in the gospel. The message is clear. Paul puts himself under obligation to everyone in order to win more. He wins them not by insisting on some abstract standard of behavior but by accommodating himself until they are won over to the good news. The rest of the letter applies his Christian standards to those who have been won over. This statement of principles is intended to assert a difference between his attitude and the attitudes of other apostles with whom he is being compared by the right wing.

Although that much is clear, there is another intriguing feature in this statement. This all occurs in the midst of a defense of Paul's apostleship, inserted into his discussion of Corinthian ethical and behavioral difficulties. Should this principle of accommodation be applied to the Corinthians as well, or does Paul intend it to be limited to himself alone? Certainly here it applies to Paul alone. There is not a hint in I Cor., ch. 9, that anyone else is included. The train of thought begins in 9:1, "Am *I* not an apostle?" and concludes consistently with the first person singular (9:23, 27). Even the inclusion of Barnabas with Paul (9:6ff.) seems to be left behind when he gets to v. 15. On the strength of ch. 9 we would be forced to say that this is a peculiarly apostolic principle, and applies therefore to Paul and to such other apostles as agreed with its basic premise.

The question can be redefined by referring once again to 10:31 to 11:1. In vs. 31–32 the subject of the statements is "you." In v. 33 Paul changes to the first person singular, summarizing quite effectively all that he has said in 9:19–23 about himself. And in 11:1 he reverts to "you" again. He appears to have some unease about applying to everyone the principle that he himself adopts. For he advises the Corinthians to "give no offense . . ."—a passive principle—while he says of himself, "As I try to please"—a more active standard of behavior. This is partly reflected in Rom. 14:13 and 15:2, in both of which cases it is also passive.

A distinction can be detected, then, between what Paul is inclined to say of himself and what he feels about everyone else in Corinth. If his language is carefully, though unconsciously, chosen, he is asserting an active principle of accommodation for himself and only a more passive form for others. Nonetheless, this subtlety should not obscure the fact that Paul is prepared to recommend that the Corinthians model themselves on his own principle. So we must conclude that he envisages something of the same kind of freedom for them as for himself.

We should be hesitant to claim too much for his view of freedom in I Corinthians, since he does not repeat exactly this view elsewhere. He does state a number of times his basic view of Christian freedom (e.g., Gal. 5:1ff.; Col. 2:16ff.; Rom. 14:1ff.; etc.). Generally he says that one is not to offend, not to judge, not to be judged by others, and so on. He allows for an adaptability on the part of the Christians at Corinth, as we shall see in the next chapter, but this is not the major focus. The emphasis remains upon himself and his behavior.

The reason for this is partly the notion of apostolicity with which Paul works. His missionary activity is an apostolic labor which, when rightly understood, calls for a degree of flexibility. Within the churches founded by apostles a similar need is still present, but in a more passive way. A second reason is that though the church in Corinth needs more than its share of adaptability it is not a situation in which it would be helpful for Christians deliberately to emulate the more radical views of behavior adopted by some.

For these two reasons Paul shies away from a simple straightforward inclusion of everyone in his principle of adaptability. This part of the study has dealt with Paul's advice to his congregations, in particular to the church at Corinth. There is another side to this question—Paul's attitude toward other apostles and their freedom to be accommodating.

4. PAUL AND PETER

Paul claimed quite deliberately to be able to adjust his practice to suit his constituency. To admit this as openly as he does requires remarkable confidence. Inconsistency in the Christian life is rarely looked upon favorably, even in a missionary situation. To state it as a principle, indeed as *the* principle, is bold indeed. Lest there be misunderstanding, it should be underscored that his accommodatory principle applies only to behavior. It does not apply to matters that Paul would consider to be essential to the content of the good news. On those matters Paul stands firm; on those there could be no adjustment and no compromise (e.g., Gal. 1:6–9). We are dealing not with the presentation of the gospel itself, but with the way those who present it, and those who have received it, live.

In a controversy described in II Corinthians, Paul appears to presuppose his inconsistency, though he denies the conclusions his opponents draw from it. These issues come to the fore in II Cor., chs. 10 to 13, dealing with questions about apostleship. He begins in II Cor. 10:1 by referring to some Corinthians who criticize him for being humble when present but bold when absent. A similar point is referred to in 10:10 with respect to his letters: his presence is weak but his letters are strong. This ambiguity which the Corinthians criticize is not violently rejected by Paul. Though he counters it, he does not get unduly upset. But he does compare his actions and his understanding of apostleship with those of other un-named apostles (10:12, "those who commend themselves"; 11:5, "superlative apostles"; 11:12ff., "false apostles, deceitful workmen, disguising themselves as apostles of Christ"; 11:23, "servants of Christ"; 12:11, "superlative apostles").

It is helpful to identify these persons, yet to do so with certainty is not possible. It is likely that Paul has in mind a group of apostles related to those in Gal., ch. 2, to whom he refers as "those who have a reputation" (Gal. 2:6) and "those who have a reputation as pillars" (Gal. 2:9). He names these as James and Cephas (Peter) and John. These, he says, added nothing to him (Gal. 2:6); they gave him the right hand of fellowship and agreed on the division of the mission task with Paul and Barnabas (vs. 7, 9).

It is helpful to pay close attention to the evidence of tensions and difficulties in early Christianity, for the issues can be seen most clearly when there is some difference of opinion. While older critical approaches used to drive too large a wedge between Paul and Peter in particular, we must be careful not to underestimate the differences that did exist. It is unmistakable from Galatians and from II Corinthians that there were issues both of principle and personal animus. We cannot accurately describe these in any detail, but in what follows we will attempt to trace the outlines.

An investigation of Paul's account in Gal. 2:11–14 will help to build such a picture. He says:

But when Cephas came to Antioch, I stood up to him to his face, because he was condemned. For before some from James came he ate with the Gentiles; but when they came he withdrew and separated himself, fearing those of the circumcision. And the rest of the Jews shared his insincerity, so that even Barnabas was carried away by their insincerity. But when I saw that they were not being consistent with the truth of the good news, I said to Cephas before them all, "If you a Jew live like a Gentile and not like a Jew, how can you force Gentiles to Judaize?"

This dramatic account highlights some fascinating features about early Christianity. The most obvious is Paul's claim that Peter's behavior is like his own: both are eating with Gentiles, both are living *not as Jews.* In other words, both are adaptable to the particular situation of the Antioch congregation. Peter is acting in a way that conforms to Paul's statement in I Cor., ch. 9—or so Paul says. He behaves as one not under law in order to keep the church together. Paul accuses both his close friend Barnabas and Peter of acting insincerely. For when a delegation (or is it only a casual visit?) of "some from James" comes to Antioch, the two of them change their behavior. By now James has assumed the dominant leadership role in Jerusalem. Has he sent a delegation to Antioch to enforce a stricter form of behavior? Or have some from James simply arrived and attempted to cajole Peter and Barnabas into adopting their standards? We shall never know, though the latter seems more likely. In any event, under pressure from these persons and because of fear of the circumcised, Peter and Barnabas and the rest of the Jews cease eating with the uncircumcised Gentile Christians.

Paul is scandalized by this behavior, because it will leave his Gentile converts in an impossible position. But what of Peter? Try viewing it through Peter's eyes to see how it looks to him. Peter is an apostle to the circumcised. He, like Paul, travels extensively to carry out this mission. Before long he has ministered in Corinth, to judge from Paul's references to him in the Corinthian letters (I Cor. 1:12; 3:10, 22; 15:5; II Cor., chs. 10 to 13), and certainly he has already visited Antioch. We may infer from I Peter 1:1 that later he has a close relationship with churches in Pontus, Galatia, Cappadocia, Asia, and Bithynia, perhaps also as a result of visits. He is portrayed by Luke as the first one to accept the possibility of Gentiles becoming Christians without circumcision (Acts, chs. 10 to 11). His credentials as a missionary are thus impeccable, and he has probably reached a view with respect to missionary activity somewhat similar to that of Paul: behave in specific situations as the need demands. In Antioch show your oneness with that church by eating with the Gentiles.

However, Peter is unlike Paul in two important related respects. First, Peter is an apostle first and foremost to the Jewish people, to the circumcised. Paul's concern for the Gentiles puts one pressure on Paul, but Peter's concern for the Jew weights things differently for him. Different forms of behavior will seem appropriate to these two servants of Christ. Second, for Peter, Jerusalem is the center of his missionary activity. In Jerusalem was found the core of conservatism in the early church. That is not to say that all Christians in Jerusalem were conservative; but those elements in Jerusalem which were intensely concerned for the continuing contact between Jewish Christians and Jews in Judea held a much more conservative view of Christianity than Paul, whose work was primarily in the Diaspora. It is indisputable that Paul shared that concern (see Chapter I, sections 4 and 6), but the different cultural and religious setting in which he worked forced him to a different expression of it. This concern is evident in Acts 21:20-26 and in Paul's collection for the poor saints in Jerusalem.

James was held in high regard by Jerusalem Jews (see Josephus, *Antiquities of the Jews,* 20.9.1), even while he was leader of the church in Jerusalem. So it was no accident that the pressure group described in Galatians was associated, rightly or wrongly, with James. This group's concern was legitimate: How can they maintain a reasonable interface between themselves and non-Christian Jews if Peter is known to be inconsistent in Antioch? The example of the leading apostle of the circumcision was important in Jerusalem. It is easy to imagine a powerful plea to Peter, asking him for the good of the gospel, no less, to withdraw from this table fellowship so that the ministry of James and the others in Jerusalem will not be compromised. Peter might well say to himself that eating with uncircumcised Gentiles is not in itself wrong, but that under the present circumstances it is more important that he accommodate himself to Jerusalem than to Antioch. That, after all, is where his task lies. If he should cut himself off from the other apostles to the circumcision, he might end up in a no-man's-land.

The Jerusalem Christians represented a variety of views. We should not oversimplify and identify all Jerusalem Christians as necessarily conservative. Amid the various viewpoints that existed there, Peter was on the left; but since those with the more radical views that had been present earlier had been forced out with the death of Stephen and the persecution that followed, we may imagine that the range was not as wide as in other places. Peter's affinities and responsibilities, at the time in question, all lie in Jerusalem. So the pressure on him from Jerusalem must be taken seriously even when he is in Antioch.

It may be that Peter's relationship with Jerusalem eventually became strained to the breaking point over these questions and that he did become less closely tied to Jerusalem.

For not only did James become the leader in Jerusalem, but Peter's name became associated with the northerly parts of Asia Minor (I Peter 1:1). Did he perhaps move away from Jerusalem into an itinerant ministry like Paul's because his position in Jerusalem had been undercut through the conflicting pressures?

At any event, Peter was disturbed by a conflict over his priorities. How should he act when the good of two groups was at stake? As he saw it, it was far more important to be inconsistent before the Antioch church, to run the risk of appearing hypocritical, than not to conform to the Jerusalem views. So strong were the arguments and so convincing the case that Barnabas and others, maybe a majority, followed suit. Paul was left at an almost empty table, pondering a case that may not have been as convincing as he had thought.

Thus it is illuminating that in the letter to the Galatians, Paul talked about pleasing men just as in I Cor. 10:31 to 11:1. The difference is that in Gal. 1:10 he rejected completely the idea of pleasing men! At Corinth he saw his task as pleasing men in everything, even if he was inconsistent. In Galatia he refused to please men, for this was inconsistent with being a servant of Christ. There are two reasons for this. One is that he associated the contentious question with the content of the gospel, though it was raised simply through a behavioral question. The other reason may be found in the immediate circumstances of the incident that took place at Antioch when Peter may have argued that in order to be accommodating and to please men he must withdraw.

This understanding of Peter's actions at Antioch can be pressed one step further, to see the full scope of the problem. When Paul went to Jerusalem with the collection for the poor (Acts, ch. 21), he was faced with a request to accommodate himself to Jewish customs. Paul agreed to the request. It was important when he was in Jerusalem to live like a Jew—

important both for his own sake and, more particularly, for the sake of the Jerusalem church.

Now, what would happen if a group of Christians from Galatia or Antioch had come to Jerusalem just at the time Paul was undertaking the Nazirite vow in Jerusalem? What would Paul do? He would be in a double bind, exactly like Peter's in Antioch. To continue with his vow might undercut his ministry to the Gentiles; to abandon it would undercut his credibility in Jerusalem.

Fortunately or unfortunately such a situation did not arise for Paul. But it did for Peter. His choice was determined by his primary concern: the mission to the circumcised. Paul in Jerusalem may likewise have chosen his first concern, the mission to the uncircumcised.

If this is anywhere near the mark, why was Paul so upset in Antioch? One could too readily say that it was because he was blind to the possibility of similar situations being forced on him. More likely, Paul was angry because Peter was in Paul's territory. There was a kind of territorial imperative, for we know that the missionary activity had been divided, even though we do not know exactly how (Gal. 2:7–10). We know that Paul at this time (though perhaps not later) had a special relationship to the Antioch church. Peter was on his ground, and so should defer, should continue deferring, to practice that was customary in Antioch. Even when faced with a pressing demand from Jerusalem, Paul deemed it important that the practice of the Gentile churches should not be subverted, especially when a matter like circumcision was at stake. Circumcision *as a principle* had already been given up by Peter (Acts, chs. 10 to 11) and even James (if we accept Acts 15:5, 19–21, 28–29, though the council likely postdates the Antioch incident). Hence Peter should adapt to Antioch, said Paul, not to Jerusalem. The apostolic agreement required this.

So, Paul in Jerusalem deferred to that church's practice. His principle of apostolic freedom demanded that of him in deference to Peter and James and John. He did not hesitate to live as a Jew when it helped to win his fellow Jews to the gospel. But Peter should defer to the Antioch church's practice in similar fashion. Missionary apostles should be flexible. It is part and parcel of their freedom.

5. CONCLUSION

Some summary statements on these questions will provide a conclusion:

a. Law is no way to solve the problem of Christian behavior; Spirit is the motivating force for all Christian life.

b. Important as the Holy Spirit is, because Christians are involved in a struggle they still need advice from more mature Christians. So Paul gives a lot of advice and encouragement, sometimes even commands, to help them follow Jesus more closely.

c. The goal of Christians is to become imitators of Christ. If imitating someone like Paul helps, by all means they are to do so.

d. Because of the wide range of ethical dilemmas facing the Christian community, a Christian may not stand firmly on simple absolute patterns of behavior in matters unimportant to the gospel. Instead, the Christian should pursue a more flexible principle: do not give offense, do not erect stumbling blocks, try to be accommodating. This passive principle applies to all.

e. For himself Paul goes even further: apostolic activity requires an active principle of accommodation that verges on being totally inconsistent. This principle defers to the yet more important goal "to save some."

f. When conflicts arise between competing demands, as

happened to Peter at Antioch and to Paul at Jerusalem, one should show a primary concern for the people present, not for the people back home. Similarly, when a conflict arises between apostles over such matters, one gives in to the other on the other's home ground.

g. Thus apostolic freedom is not to be curtailed simply by the pressures from more conservative fellow Christians. Indeed, it is not a matter of conservative or liberal at all; it depends upon the truth of the gospel and the needs of the community.

h. Apostolic freedom is, first and foremost, freedom of an apostle—a freedom drawn from the risen Jesus for the task to which the apostle is commissioned. But because the gospel is a gospel of freedom, and because all things are lawful, it is a freedom that may be shared by all in their pursuit of the imitation of Christ.

It is a widely held view that Christians are legalistic and hidebound. We who identify ourselves as Christians do not like the thrust of that criticism, but we are forced to accept its general validity. Frequently that tendency to arbitrary courses of action is linked with a lack of concern for others, an insensitivity to the effect of our legalism on others. Paul's notion of flexibility opens up an alternative, one that can be linked with the operative principle of love, yet without ever losing sight of the real goal of Christianity.

V

Love and License

PAUL WAS being pushed in two directions. Some wanted to push him to the right, to a conservative view of the theology and practice of freedom. Some wanted to push him farther left. The Christian community in Jerusalem often expressed the first point of view. Some of the Hellenistic churches expressed the more liberal understanding of freedom, which was less concerned to "conserve" the association with Judaism. They wished to force some of the important Christian insights to their logical conclusions. From left and right Paul's position was called into question. He attempted to walk a tightrope between the dangers looming on each side. To a large extent he was successful. He recognized what was valid theologically in each of the competing tendencies, often accepting the rationale of one side and the practice of the other. For example, he accepted the rationale of the left about food, but the practice of the right. At another time he accepted the rationale of the right about women in worship but the practice of the left.

That overly neat schematization is not always true. Each of the churches that Paul founded was different. Simple "left" and "right" categories are not always accurate; they are useful insofar as they connote alternatives to Paul's position. Thus, the theology and practice of some Christians in

Galatia who stood to Paul's "right" might have relatively little in common with the views of other Christians elsewhere who might also stand to Paul's "right." It is still a highly controversial question to what extent there was similarity of outlook among the various opinions opposed to Paul's in his scattered churches. The particular circumstances and makeup of the church, together with variations in the cultural and religious milieu, have a considerable effect upon the way opinions coalesce.

One other *caveat* is necessary. The word "group" will be used frequently as a convenience. This is not meant to imply that there were neatly defined groups of Christians in Paul's churches that were for him or against him. It is much more likely that the "groups" were constantly shifting, depending upon the issue in question. There were probably no leaders of groups, though in the Corinthian situation certain key Christians—Paul, Apollos, Cephas—were being claimed as leaders. What characterized these "groups" were similarities of outlook, theological perspective, openness or restrictiveness. Underneath all this, it is still abundantly clear that the early Christian communities were faced with considerable conflict.

1. WISDOM IN CORINTH

In Corinth some features of conflict are relatively clear. We know that there are factions in the church (I Cor. 1: 10–13; 3:3–9; 4:6; 11:17–19), and that these are more fully developed than in the other congregations for which we have evidence, though we are not able to say exactly what the distinctive characteristics of each faction are. We know too that there are major ethical problems, and that these ethical questions were a matter of dispute between Paul and Corinth. There was a previous letter from Paul (I Cor. 5:9) and a communication from Corinth to Paul (I Cor. 7:1), in addition to which there have been visits (I Cor. 1:11; 16:3, 10, 12). The Corinthian correspondence that remains is only partial evidence for a set of difficulties that extended over several years, at least, and probably included other questions we now know nothing about. However, we know more about Corinth than about any of the other churches, and so it is proper to begin here.

In Corinth, Paul is being pressed from both left and right. Some urge a radical view of freedom, some a more conservative position. Paul's view, as enunciated in I Corinthians, is not just a middle-of-the-road position. Sometimes he agrees with one group, sometimes with another. He agrees with the slogan of the left—indeed, he may even have coined it—that "all things are lawful." This basic acceptance of a liberal view should not be minimized. But he disagrees with them in their practice of freedom. He does not agree with the fundamental attitude of the conservatives toward freedom, but he does argue for care and concern and a restriction on the exercise of freedom. Essentially Paul's view is that Christians must adopt a constructive ethical stance. Whatever destroys another person's relationship with God or with others is not acceptable.

The forces pushing to the left in Corinth posit the most sensitive questions. Some of the left-wingers go so far that they may be called radicals in their view of freedom, but it is a stance that is supported by a claim to be the most spiritual ones in the congregation. Insofar as this is true, it makes their position especially interesting.

The earliest indication of trouble is found in Paul's references to "wisdom," beginning with I Cor. 1:17, where he contrasts the preaching of the cross with "eloquent wisdom." To view the message about Jesus as a type of "wisdom" has pernicious effects which need to be countered. Thus he quotes

Isa. 29:14 (in I Cor. 1:19) as a first argument against wisdom: it will be destroyed by God. Christian experience demonstrates that those who believe the gospel do so on the basis of preaching, a foolish activity and not an exercise in wisdom (see 1:21; cf. 1:22–25). Further, he points out that not even the Corinthians can really claim to be wise, so they should not base their salvation on something they don't even possess (1:26–31). Lastly, not even Paul boasts in his wisdom; he relies entirely on the power of the Spirit (2:1–5).

All of this is negative and polemical. Wisdom is wrong because it undercuts the way in which God works. In 2:6 the tone changes; the mood is still polemical, but Paul aims at a take-over of the idea of wisdom. He admits that in fact he *does* speak wisdom, in spite of his arguments to this point. What is even more confusing, he says that he uses wisdom among the "mature" or "fully developed" (2:6), a term used by those who value wisdom. This wisdom is spoken "in a mystery," for it is a "hidden" wisdom (2:7). It is different, however, from that of the "rulers of this age which is passing away" (2:6; cf. 2:8). They cannot know the kind of wisdom Paul is talking about. In short, Paul argues against wisdom, then admits his use of wisdom, and then attempts to distinguish between the two kinds of wisdom.

Now the description in 2:6–8 sounds very much like the position of some of Paul's opponents in Corinth. The ideas have rather marked affinities with two kinds of thought: contemporary Hellenistic Judaism and later Gnosticism. On the one hand, Hellenistic Judaism had in some places developed by this time a view of "wisdom" that came almost to replace God. Wisdom was becoming hypostatized; that is, an attribute of God was elevated to a position of such prominence that it could stand for the whole of God's activity. In this fashion, wisdom could be seen as the operative principle in creation, the sum of the knowledge of God, and even a means of redemption (see Prov., ch. 8; Wisd. of Sol., ch. 7; Ecclus., ch. 24). These ideas of wisdom within Judaism can be understood to a large extent as developments that sought to avoid direct reference to God but still give him the primary place. But in so doing, the traditional view of God was subtly changed.

On the other hand, we can trace a line of development later than the New Testament period in which "wisdom" is used as one of the key concepts of Gnostic Christianity (from *gnosis,* "knowledge"). Some varieties of Gnosticism can be traced to the middle of the second century, and evidence for some similar views can be found in the New Testament, though without the later systematic development. According to these views, one needs to acquire secret knowledge before one can attain salvation. *Sophia,* or wisdom, becomes a semidivine agent of redemption and mediation between God and man. The general question that confronts the student of the New Testament is the extent to which its echoes of gnosticizing ideas should be interpreted in the light of the later developments.

This problem is posed in an acute form in I Corinthians. Is the use of these ideas evidence of "Gnosticism" in Corinth? Why is "wisdom" so prominently displayed in Corinth? Is Paul a Gnostic? It is not possible to enter into this debate here, but it will be helpful to sketch out the likeliest solution. It is probable that a group of Christians in Corinth has been deeply affected by a Hellenistic Jewish hypostatizing of wisdom as a means of redemption. With this it has allied other Greek philosophical speculations about the role of wisdom. The Corinthian problem should not be termed Gnostic or Gnosticism; those terms should be reserved for the second and third centuries. Instead, it is useful to adopt the term "gnosticizing" or "proto-gnostic" for this Corinthian theology, for there seems to be a great debt to speculative modes of thought centering around "wisdom" and "knowledge." This theology is syncretistic in that it borrows from more than one religious framework, attempting to blend diverse ideas into a harmonious whole. No doubt the Corinthian supporters of these ideas would say that they were merely interacting with their culture. They have taken *gnosis* ("knowledge") and *sophia* ("wisdom") from the Jewish and Greek worlds and have applied them in an almost mystical fashion to Christ.

A hundred or so years later these early developments will become fused with other alien features and produce what we now know as Gnosticism. Though that system of thought ought not to be used to interpret the Corinthian situation, it is the logical conclusion to the sort of development that was taking place in one part of the Corinthian congregation.

Against this view Paul has first of all repudiated the basic approach (1:17–25) and then attempted to counter their thrust by adopting some of the terminology and changing the content. This is a standard technique of Paul's. In at least two other congregations where somewhat similar tendencies seem to be at work—Philippi and Colossae—he does the same thing. The most notable instance is the great Christ-hymn in Col. 1:15–20, where somewhat alien terminology is baptized into Christian thought. Paul's willingness to bend in the matter of concepts and word usage is worth noting. At the same time, he deliberately retains the distinctive emphasis of the atonement, so that he never lets go the ideas that Jesus was really flesh and really died for man's redemption.

The radical group in Corinth may be described as proto-gnostic. It has hewn the majority of its building blocks from Hellenistic Judaism and Greek philosophy. In I Cor. 2:6ff. Paul takes over the idea of wisdom and applies it to Jesus as the wisdom of God revealed by the Spirit. He draws a sharp line between God's revelation through wisdom and revelation through Spirit (2:10–16). Wisdom, as applied to Jesus, is totally other than the wisdom of the rulers of this age (a gnosticizing concept), though Paul calls it a mystery and one intended for the mature (both concepts that play a large role in late gnostic systems).

Against this glorified idea of "wisdom," Paul asserts the hard, cold reality of history: the Lord of glory was crucified (2:8). This idea, repugnant to anyone tainted with too alien an understanding of the way of redemption, is made even more unattractive by the association he makes between the mind of the Lord and the mind of Christ (2:16). A group is beginning to form which holds an esoteric doctrine of wisdom, in which the offense of the fleshly existence and real crucifixion of Jesus Christ is evacuated of its significance. As these persons develop the implications of wisdom for redemption, they will have to consider the implications for ethics as well. If one's relationship to God is assured on the basis of one's insight, one may be tempted to adopt radical views of behavior. In fact, this seems to have been the case. A radical view of freedom develops on the basis of their view of wisdom or knowledge (see I Cor. 8:1, 2, 7, 10). Even though Paul agrees that all things are lawful, he bases his view on the premise that law has been transcended by the grace of Christ, not on *gnosis*.

2. THE RADICAL POSITION

That a "wisdom" group existed in Corinth is highly likely. This group becomes real from the discussion of ethical problems in I and II Corinthians. It may be that no member of the group was affected by all the problems raised in the letters, but the general impression is that the problems were created by a group of persons all of whom work from the same set of assumptions. We will attempt to sort out some of the characteristics of this group.

First of all, they are claiming to possess a special wisdom that makes them "spiritual"; the uninitiated are "fleshly." In their view, all depends upon one's knowledge. Paul counters this by claiming that those who depend upon the Spirit are spiritual; they have the mind of Christ. The opponents are fleshly (I Cor. 2:12–16; cf. I Cor. 12:1ff.; and 15:44–50, where the contrast is related to the question of resurrection). For both Paul and his opponents, to be spiritual is good, to be of the flesh is bad. But the question is whether the spiritual originates in wisdom or in Spirit. Paul insists that it is the latter (see II Cor., ch. 3).

They seem also to claim some special knowledge of the "rulers of the world" (I Cor. 2:6–8; II Cor. 4:4). This implies a view that multiple spiritual forces are affecting the destinies of persons (cf. the "elemental spirits of the universe" in Gal. 4:3 and Col. 2:8). If so, an alien—though common—idea has penetrated into this Christian congregation, probably from the East.

More seriously, they are denying the future resurrection of the body (I Cor. 15:12–13). Paul rejects this absolutely. If they are correct, he claims, then Jesus has not been raised and the bottom drops out of the Christian faith (I Cor. 15:14–19). It is unlikely that this group is saying that there is *no* resurrection, but rather that the resurrection has taken place already. Christians are as transformed as they can be through the resurrection of Jesus; the body has been fully redeemed. If so, deviant behavior then becomes acceptable (cf. I Cor. 15:34). It does not matter very much now what one does with the body. Paul's answer to this is that there is a future resurrection when Christians will be completely transformed (I Cor. 15:35–50). Because it is a future event, behavior now is vitally important.

The radical group also has a deficient understanding of the

Spirit, and this makes a travesty of Christian ethics. Paul's basic position is that all Christians are filled with the Spirit (I Cor. 3:16–17); behavior that is not the carrying out of the Spirit's impulse is invalid (e.g., I Cor. 12:3). Ethics is a basic test of the reality of Christian experience. The opponents, however, are pursuing visions, strange tongues, revelations, and other spiritual gifts (I Cor., chs. 12 to 14) as the test of Christian experience. In their concentration on these they fall into the error of spiritual pride, which goes hand in hand with the failure to be concerned for behavior. Against this Paul presumes to set his own experience (II Cor. 12:1–10; I Cor. 14:18–19).

Since they claim that the Spirit has fully come and that the resurrection has fully occurred, they can claim to be "reigning" already. The Kingdom of God is fully introduced here and now. Paul deals with this claim sarcastically (I Cor. 4:8–10) when he expresses the wish to be reigning with them. He also comments ironically on the role of apostles, who by comparison with the pneumatics appear to be nothing. By the time II Cor., chs. 10 to 13, was written the question of apostleship had become the single most important issue. However, it is not certain that the trouble arose from exactly the same group that gave rise to his pained comments earlier (I Cor. 4:9–20).

Many of the traits described above are akin to later views of *gnōsis.* The less intense and still unintegrated form of these views in the Corinth of Paul's day justifies the use of the word "proto-gnostic" for the group with which Paul is fighting. Paul's essential argument against them is the reality of the death and resurrection of Jesus (I Cor. 15:3–11; cf. 1:23; 1:18; 2:8; II Cor. 1:9; 4:14; 5:14–15; etc.). Where Paul historicizes the good news, they spiritualize it (in the wrong sense) by idealizing and interiorizing the means of redemption, the future hope, and the way of access to God. Paul is never unmindful of this "spiritual" dimension, as his stress on the Spirit demonstrates. But where his opponents appear to sever the connection between Jesus and the Spirit, Paul holds on to the connection between them.

One important feature of this disjunction between the Spirit and Jesus, between spirit and flesh, is their ethical stance. If the resurrection has happened, if knowledge of God is disembodied and idealized, then what happens in the body is much less important. Only if this life, this body, and the *future* transformation of this body are taken seriously, can behavior be given its proper place. Too great an emphasis on the spiritual can result in a spurious notion of liberty. In such a view it would be legitimate to keep on sinning so that God's grace would seem much more profound (cf. Rom. 6:1, 12, 15). Though that slogan does not appear in Corinthians, the conditions are ripe for it. In fact, the slogan may well be present in Paul's letter to the Romans as a reflection of the ethical problems he had only recently faced in Corinth. We turn now to these left-wing problems encouraged by the conglomeration of proto-gnostic, Hellenistic Jewish, and Christian ideas of wisdom, redemption, and resurrection. They all relate in some fashion to the legitimate exercise of freedom.

3. ETHICAL PROBLEMS

In sketching the problems that the left presents for Paul, we should note, in all fairness to the Corinthians, that in many cases they raise the problem by asking for his advice. It is worthwhile noting, too, that these same problems do not recur in II Corinthians. Whether the challenge to Paul altered so much that he did not wish to raise the ethical questions again or whether his first letter was sufficiently persuasive is not clear. In any case, no further light is shed on most of these in the later correspondence.

The first and most painful problem was sexual immorality. One of the Corinthian Christians was sleeping either with his mother or with his mother-in-law. Bad as such antinomianism was, the reaction of the church was even worse. Arrogantly the members tolerated this behavior (I Cor. 5:1–2) as if it needed no decisive response. Perhaps they even boasted (5:2, 6) about their willingness to accept everything in the name of "wisdom." They have neglected the importance of Jesus' Lordship (5:4–5). They have confused a legitimate refusal to judge everyone outside the church—to do that would also be arrogant—with the legitimate need to judge what goes on within the Christian community. To refuse to do that is unacceptable laxity (5:9–13). Paul had already referred to this problem in an earlier letter (5:9).

The second problem that Paul has learned about (perhaps from Chloe's family, I Cor. 1:11) is that some Christians are taking fellow Christians to court (6:1–8). They are asking pagans to settle disputes between Christians (6:1) when in fact there ought to be no disputes at all between believers (6:7). Since the world itself is going to be judged by Christians (6:2–4), it is absurd to allow the judges of this world to judge the brotherhood. The crowning touch is that Christians are wronging and defrauding their own brothers in Christ (6:8), making a mockery of their sanctification—even of their justification—in the name of the Lord Jesus Christ and in the Spirit of God (6:11).

The third problem is described after a reference to the slogan "All things are lawful for me" (I Cor. 6:12). This self-conscious concern for freedom is a feature of the gnosticizing party. Libertarianism is the issue. Making use of the services of a prostitute (6:13–18) is a deliberate assertion of the gnosticizing principle that the body is not terribly important; what matters is one's knowledge or wisdom. Since all things are lawful, since it is the body's natural state to desire evil (see Rom. 7:13–25; cf. Rom., ch. 6; Gal. 5:13–21), and since man's sexual appetite demands sex just as the stomach needs food (I Cor. 6:13), what is wrong with a bit of old-fashioned bodily indulgence? The body is hardly the central matter on which salvation stands or falls; it is the Spirit that really matters, and the Corinthians can claim to have the Spirit (6:17–19).

The fourth problem—marriage—begins the discussion of questions about which they wrote (I Cor. 7:1). The question is whether marriage is still appropriate in the time after Jesus has come (7:1–2). One should remember that Jesus said that in the resurrection there is no marriage (Matt. 22:30) and also, in answer to a question about the expediency of marriage, that being a eunuch is best for those who can accept it (Matt. 19:10–12). The Corinthian enthusiasts are claiming *this* as the resurrection time, and some of them are urging that it would be appropriate for a man not to touch a woman. This view is troubling marriages: some partners are refusing sexual intercourse on spiritual grounds (I Cor. 7:3–7). Separations are occurring for this reason (7:10–11) and also because of the unbelief of one of the partners (7:12–16). When this problem is put alongside the earlier ones of immorality and prostitution, it becomes apparent that the church is being pulled both toward asceticism on the one hand and toward libertarian indulgence on the other.

When Paul deals specifically with the unmarried it is apparent that he is out on his own limb (I Cor. 7:25). The problem is: Would it be a sin to seek a change in one's marital status (7:27–40)? Should marriages be sought? What will be a husband's or a wife's priorities? What if one is already engaged? What about widows? These special questions are all troubling. They too represent the opposite of the license involved in seeking out prostitutes. Here we have more evidence of a trend toward asceticism, which seeks to downgrade the need for the satisfaction of sexual desires.

The fifth problem, having to do with eating food offered to idols, is introduced by another of the proto-gnostics' slogans: "We all possess knowledge" (I Cor. 8:1). Part of that knowledge is that "an idol has no real existence" (8:4) since there is only one true God. There are no other gods and lords (8:4–6). But Paul presents a more subtle case: some have been accustomed to eating idol food and have not yet been liberated in Christ from thinking that a real god is associated with the food (8:7–10). If a Christian who is liberated were to eat in an idol's temple (8:10), it could be devastating to the newly converted Christian (8:11–13).

If we jump over ch. 9 and the first half of ch. 10 of I Corinthians (see Chapter IV), we find that the same problem begins again in 10:14 (especially 10:19ff.). Paul appears to have second thoughts: no matter how mature one might be, there is still a danger in eating this idol food (10:20–22). He repeats the old slogan "All things are lawful" and then raises a different facet of the problem: What about buying meat in the market? Will not the one with a tender conscience have to stop eating (10:25–26)? And what about private dinner parties (10:27–30)? These social and culinary questions are potentially divisive, though Paul's treatment of them suggests that he is raising them on his own as an expansion of the actual question of 8:1.

The sixth problem is dealt with in a backhanded way. In I Cor. 11:2, Paul commends the Corinthians for maintaining the traditions he delivered to them, particularly the tradition concerning the Lord's Supper (11:23–26) and the traditional formulation of the good news (15:3–8). The issue at stake in the former is female participation in worship (11:3–16) (see Chapter III). In connection with this he quotes a traditional practice. The question about women who are praying and prophesying in church (11:16) with their heads uncovered

(11:5, 13) is presented as if the issue is not the activity itself but the dress of those so engaged (11:3–7, 10, 14–15). It is likely that, because of the traditional attitude toward women, the Jewish group in the church is offended by the practice. Christians should give no offense to Jews (10:32). It may even be that an enthusiastic group is pushing new practices, new liberties, new understandings of the relationship between male and female. They may even be quoting Paul's own slogan "In Christ there is neither male nor female." If so, by urging a complete indifference to all distinctions they may be going much farther than Paul. While perhaps correct (and Paul's essential agreement with this view might account for the complexity of the argument in this section), this attitude is not helpful to the church as a whole. It must then be countered.

With this we are fully into the communal abuses. The seventh problem dealt with by Paul is the abuse of the Lord's Supper, which has already been hinted at in I Cor. 10:16–22. Of all the ethical problems, this is the only one in which any connection is made with the divisions in the community (11:17–19). At its root the problem has to do with participation in the Lord's Supper. Some are coming too filled—with wine (11:21). Some are not filled enough—with food (11:21, 34). As a result, the body and blood of Jesus is taken unworthily (11:27) and without discernment (11:29–30). The rich have no concern for the poor; both are thereby prevented from adequate participation in the remembrance of Christ's death.

The eighth ethical difficulty continues church-related questions. This time it concerns spiritual gifts, or perhaps those who claim to be spiritual (*pneumatikoi* in I Cor. 12:1 may mean either gifts or people, though in 12:4 it is clear that "gifts," *charismata,* are in mind). The test of a person is whether he utters the standard Christian confession "Jesus is

Lord" (12:3). It may be that the proto-gnostics are claiming that the Spirit actually is inspiring them to say *"Jesus* is anathema," that *Christ* is all. If so, the point is to denigrate the bodily nature of the Jesus of history (cf. also II Cor. 5:16f.). However that may be, within the group of those who make a Christian confession there will be considerable variety but in each person the Spirit will be working (12:4–31). Some Corinthians, not recognizing the necessity of all gifts, are claiming higher or better gifts. The reality is that since all gifts have the same origin, there can be no question of superiority. It is the same Spirit (12:4), the same Lord (12:5), the same God (12:6; cf. also vs. 8, 9, 11, 13). The view that some exercise lesser gifts (12:23–24) must be rejected if the community is to see itself as the body of Christ (12:12–27). The assumed superiority of some continues to be the polemical focus of I Cor., ch. 13. Speaking in tongues (13:1, 8), prophecy, mysteries, *gnōsis,* faith (13:2, 8) and asceticism (13:3) all are being claimed as a higher "way" (12:31; 14:1).

Two of these issues are picked up and dealt with at length: speaking in tongues and prophesying (I Cor., ch. 14). These we shall look at more carefully later (see Chapter VII). Here we need only reinforce the contention that the problems are being created by those who are "zealous of spirits" (or "zealous of the things of the Spirit" perhaps, 14:12). The ones who claim to be prophets or spiritual (14:37) are creating problems for the church; they should heed carefully what Paul is saying to them (14:37–38).

In short, the problems arising out of the Corinthian community cover a wide range of behavior, but most come from the radical side. One exception may be the marital issue, but even it is explicable on the hypothesis of an enthusiastic gnosticizing party. A radical may go either to an extreme libertarian view or to an extreme ascetic view. A similar bifurcation can be traced in second-century gnosticism. In

any event it seems reasonably certain that a group of pneumatics see themselves as more spiritual, more in tune with the
mysteries of God, more filled with knowledge and wisdom,
more favored by God and therefore better able to sit loose to
questions affecting the body and the future state of believers.
Sexual relations with a prostitute, sexual liberties with one's
mother (-in-law?), marital questions, food offered to idols,
traditional distinctions between male and female, neglect of
the poor, abuse of the Lord's Supper, ordinary gifts—all of
these are immaterial to the spiritualists, the proto-gnostics.
They are operating on the basis of higher principles, unen-
cumbered by the demands of earthly living. All things are
lawful because all have knowledge!

4. PAUL'S RESPONSES

How does Paul answer these problems and advise the
church at large? The main lines of his attitude to ethical
questions may be set out under four topics: *(a)* traditional
Christian convictions; *(b)* the group's self-understanding;
(c) concern for others; and *(d)* advice that deals primarily
with oneself.

a. Traditional Convictions

Some of Paul's advice is based on factors that are characteristic simply of the Christian belief that the new time has
dawned. Three of these should be noted.

First, Paul draws upon the common conviction that the
end is near to push the Corinthians toward the desired kind
of behavior. This argument is applied to the question of
marriage, in both I Cor. 7:26 and 7:29. The point is that the
nearness of the end, with its impending distress, should motivate Christians to stay single, on the one hand, and to live
within marriage as if they were not married, on the other

hand. So quickly is the world expected to pass away (7:31) that the normal order of relationships and values needs to be suspended in favor of the incomparably more important set of priorities surrounding the end (cf. 10:11).

The second general approach that Paul draws on is early Christian tradition. This may seem surprising in the light of his extremely strong emphasis on Spirit, and the Spirit's supersession of traditional understandings of the law. Although tradition is not often expressed as a major factor for Paul, he draws on it at least four times: (1) In connection with women's activity in church, Paul says that he recognizes no other practice, nor do the churches of God (I Cor. 11:16); (2) when he reverts to the same matter in 14:33, he uses the same answer; (3) when dealing with abuses of the Lord's Supper, he quotes traditional (and foundational) formulas (11:23–26); and (4) when countering the arguments of the enthusiasts over the nature of the resurrection, he likewise uses a traditional formula as the authoritative proof of the reality of the bodily resurrection (15:3–8). Each time the appeal to common traditions is intended to undercut a pneumatic stress on innovation or direct knowledge of proper conduct.

A third method of approach is Paul's rather complicated Scriptural argument in I Cor. 11:2–16 and 10:1–13. In both instances, concerning women and food, a rather tortuous exegesis is used to make his case. Each time the train of thought is not completely clear. Our inability to follow Paul accurately may be a result of our lack of understanding of the context, or it may be a result of his eagerness to use every device available to him. It is certain, however, that recourse was often had to rabbinic methods of expounding Scripture which are unfamiliar to us. The Christian groups had to search for adequate tools: many they found at hand in Judaism.

b. The Christian Group

Paul has a clear view of how the church ought to understand itself. Paul's view in I Cor. 12:12–30 is that there is one body, made up of many members, all united in Christ—whether Jews or Greeks, slaves or free (and note that male and female are missing!). The Christian group is not just a body, it is the body of Christ (12:27). Though each person may have a different gift and a different role to play, all gifts are by the same Spirit, from the same God, and for the same Lord (12:4–11). Spiritual gifts are for the corporate good (chs. 12 to 14). Earlier, when discussing individual behavior, Paul uses similar language applied to the individual. The Christian's body is a member of Christ (6:15), a temple of the Holy Spirit (6:17, 19). So the individual is to glorify God in his body (6:20), just as the church is to glorify God in its several parts.

The goal of the group's worship should therefore be to build up the body, to edify and to strengthen it (I Cor. 14:3, 5, 17–19, 26), by rejecting all notions of superiority. The integrity of the body is important. Each person should remain in the state in which he first became a Christian (7:17–24), whether within marriage (vs. 12–16), concerning circumcision, or in connection with slavery (vs. 17–24; see Chapter II). A part of the underlying motivation for this may have been not to disturb the social fabric so that the proclamation of the gospel could continue without unnecessary distractions. If this is Paul's reason, his conservatism is not altogether appealing.

Given the value Paul attaches to the Christian group, two other pieces of advice become more understandable. In I Cor. 6:4–5, when dealing with the problem of lawsuits, Paul says that the church, not those outside the fellowship, ought to assume the role of judging. The church has a mediatorial role to play among its members. Even more important for Paul is the case of immorality dealt with in I Cor., ch. 5. His blunt advice is to remove the offender (5:2, 13). He is to be judged by the church, just as Paul himself has already judged him (5:3), with Paul's spirit present and with the power of the Lord Jesus (5:4–5). Though the purpose of the judgment is to save his spirit at the last day (5:5), the harsh action must be taken to safeguard the health of the group.

Paul adds another important aspect of the group's character when he stresses in I Cor., ch. 7, the mutuality of the relationship of male and female in the Christian community.

—Each man should have his own wife, each woman her own husband (7:2).
—The husband should give to his wife her conjugal rights, and likewise the wife to her husband, for the husband does not rule over his own body, nor does the wife rule over hers (7:3–4).
—Neither is to refuse the other (7:5).
—The wife should not separate from her husband, the husband should not divorce his wife (7:10–11; the difference in terminology is legally accurate for the time); the same is true for unbelieving husbands and wives (7:12–14).
—If the unbelieving partner wishes to separate, neither husband nor wife is to remain bound (7:15–16).
—The unmarried man and the unmarried woman are both anxious for the affairs of the Lord (7:32, 34), while their married counterparts are both anxious about how to please their spouses (7:33, 34).

A kind of mutuality is apparent in the question of women's participation in worship, but with a twist to make it conformable to Paul's exegesis (I Cor. 11:4–5). Head covering is important for both, but he distinguishes between male and female practices. The point is reinforced in 11:11–12, where

Paul argues that neither man nor woman is independent of the other, both are dependent on God. Such a mutual view might have gone a long way toward resolving the tensions that were developing in Paul's churches.

It is worth remarking that this mutuality is present in Romans with respect to Jews and Greeks, and in Philemon it is hinted at with respect to slaves and free (cf. also Col. 3:18 to 4:1; Eph. 5:21 to 6:9). However, important as this insight is (see Chapters I–III), it is insufficiently applied in the subsequent developments. The Christian group, which in I Corinthians is described in quite dynamic terms, becomes more stultified and fixed as time goes on (see Chapter VII). Here it is at the center of the attempt to solve the problem associated with freedom. Later it becomes the focus of the struggle for order.

c. Concern for Others

Here, too, we are at the heart of Paul's ethical advice. It can be presented in three basic principles. First, in a discussion about eating food offered to idols, Paul suggests that one should not lay any stumbling blocks or set any snares for others (I Cor. 8:7–13). To eat such food will not make any difference to the person who eats it (8:8; cf. however 10:20–21), but the assertion of such liberty might well make a difference to someone who is weak (8:9–10). The conscience of the weak man may be overly sensitive (8:12; cf. 10:28–29); still one's own knowledge should not be used as a weapon against him (8:7, 13; 10:25ff.). Yet even here Paul recognizes the possibility that a weak Christian may illegitimately attempt to control the stronger Christian's behavior through an aggressive assertion of his scruples (10:29–30). Paul's reaction to this is not certain, for the answer turns on punctuation. The usual view is that the strong Christian should not give in (see further, Chapter VI).

Second, Paul expresses the principle that one should prefer to suffer wrong oneself rather than to inflict a wrong on another (I Cor. 6:7). If a Christian takes another to court, he is too concerned for his own property and esteem. Christians are to be other-centered. A similar principle applies in the marriage situation. The believing husband or wife should not initiate a divorce or separation proceeding (7:12, 13, 15), since it is the other, and his or her possible salvation, that should be of most conern (7:16).

Third is the positive principle of seeking the good of the neighbor (I Cor. 10:24), to share with and to care for another (12:25), to wait for one another so that the other may be provided for (11:33, 21–22). This attitude is best summarized under one of Paul's favorite words: love. This is dealt with at length in I Cor., ch. 13, and is used as the summary of all his ethical teaching in the final greetings in 16:14: "Let all that you do be done in love." To this we will return.

d. Advice for Self

Though Paul does not countenance an undue concern for self, a correct concern for oneself should motivate one's behavior. Two closely related, but discrete, ideas are bound up together in I Cor. 6:12, where they are deliberately set against the radicals' slogan "All things are lawful." Paul's principles are that "not everything is helpful" and that one should "avoid becoming enslaved by anything" (cf. also 7:23). Both are negative pieces of advice. Avoid what is not going to build you up and whatever can bind you. So he advises any who cannot remain single because of difficulties and temptations to get married (7:2, 9) out of enlightened self-interest. Ultimately the motive for keeping the body pure is eschatological: the body is to be raised at the end (6:13–14), so it must be kept fit awaiting that great event (15:12–58). Linked with this is the goal of remaining free from anxiety (7:32ff.) so that one can give the Lord undivided attention (7:35).

In all the advice Paul has given to the Corinthian church his aim has been to modify the unchecked application of radical principles of behavior. The advice takes the form of qualification, redirection, consideration. One should care for self, for others, for the group; one should adhere to traditional Christian practice. It is startling, however, that Paul shies away from a fundamental attack upon radical Christian behavior. It could be that the problems are not as serious as this reconstruction suggests. But it is more likely that Paul believes that the radical stance is not itself altogether wrong. Though the reasons and the practice of the radicals may be wrong, Christian freedom is extremely broad. It needs to be qualified, but its basis and scope should not be limited. Where the radicals go dangerously wrong is in their practice. They show too little love, and eventually love is really what matters.

5. THE ROLE OF AGAPĒ

In the best-known paragraph of all of Paul's letters, I Cor., ch. 13, he develops his view of love (*agapē*). The foil for what Paul says about love is the description of the radical opponents. Their emphases are recalled again in this chapter: ecstatic experiences of tongues, prophecies, and mysteries. Their qualities are attacked: jealous, boastful, arrogant, rude, irritable, resentful, rejoicing in wrong, insisting on their own way. Love, however, is superior to all ecstatic gifts: it is the more excellent way of 12:31. Even the ascetic life is no better than the self-indulgent enthusiast (13:3). Love demonstrates a concern for the other by showing patience, kindness, trust, endurance, hope (13:4–7). Where some antagonize others and set themselves up as superior, love's way is to bear all things.

Agapē is evidence of the breaking in of the end now. The ecstatic gifts, which claim to be—and are—an irruption of the last days, will all pass away. Tongues, prophecies, knowledge, are all transitory, useful in the interim period but fated to disappear because they are imperfect. The one thing that will continue is love. It cannot end (I Cor. 13:8ff.). With such comprehensive advice and such a compelling presentation of the role of love one would optimistically hope that the Corinthian church mended its ways and went on to new heights of consistency and morality. It did not. The letter cannot have been entirely successful, for the situation deteriorated. The next phase in the correspondence is the so-called severe letter referred to in II Cor. 2:4; 7:8. We probably have a piece of this in II Cor., chs. 10 to 13, or possibly in 6:14 to 7:1. In any case, the next step was a visit from Paul's emissary Titus, who brought back some good news (II Cor. 7:6; cf. 1:23 to 2:3; 7:13–16). However, in the second and third letters to the Corinthians (now combined as II Corinthians) the focus has shifted onto Paul's self-defense, and ethical advice is almost absent. This may mean that, though I Corinthians did not solve the question of Paul's relation to the congregation, it did contribute to their better understanding of freedom, love, and adequate Christian behavior. Or it may mean simply that self-defense was so crucial that ethics had to take second place. At any event, it surfaces in the final few verses: "Mend your ways, heed my appeal, agree with one another, live in peace . . ." (II Cor. 13:11).

Even all this further contact did not solve the long-term problems. In about 95 or 96 (i.e., forty years later), Clement, bishop of Rome, wrote to the Corinthians calling them back to Paul's advice and urging them to overcome their divisions (I Clement 44, 46, 47).

6. OTHER PAULINE VIEWS

Because of its richness we have concentrated exclusively on what we can establish from Paul's Corinthian correspondence. But a quick survey of similar themes in the paraenetic sections of the other letters might be helpful.

In Galatians, Paul argues that freedom is not to be used as an opportunity for the flesh. Rather, through love Christians are to serve one another (Gal. 5:13), to love the neighbor (5:14), to walk by the Spirit (5:16) showing his fruit (5:22–23), to avoid the works of the flesh (5:16–21). If reproof is necessary, it should be gentle (6:1). Boasting is to be replaced by bearing one another's burdens (6:2–5); one should do good to all men, especially to fellow Christians (6:10). The basis for all this is the new freedom there is in Christ, a freedom based solely upon faith in him (2:15 to 4:31).

In the Thessalonian letters the problems of immorality and marriage, which also existed in Corinth, are mentioned, though they are not discussed at length (I Thess. 4:3–8). There are difficulties with a failure of some people to work —probably because of a belief in the nearness of the end— which is bringing abuse upon the Christians (I Thess. 4: 11–12; 5:14; II Thess. 3:6–13). Although love is present, more would be desirable (I Thess. 4:9–10); one must always seek to do good, and not repay evil with evil (I Thess. 5:15). The basis for adequate behavior in both Thessalonian letters is not simply faith, as in Galatians, but eschatology. All signs suggest that, though the end is not here yet, it is near. That expectation controls Paul's advice, and also accounts for the inadequate behavior of some people.

With Philippians one discovers an emphasis on oneness (Phil. 1:27), a common love (2:2), humility (2:3), and a concern for others (2:4). Following the great Christ-hymn in

2:6ff. Paul draws attention to the need for innocence and blamelessness (2:15). Later he comments on the nearness of the end (4:5) and the desirability of having no anxiety over anything (4:6). A radical group emerges, a bit obscurely, in 3:12–21. When he deals with the challenge it presents he focuses, as he does elsewhere in the letter, on Jesus. The basis of ethics is Christology.

Romans is much more difficult to summarize, and some of its themes will be developed in Chapter VI. In general, it is fair to say that Romans reflects the same kinds of advice as I Corinthians, but more softly and in more general terms. In Romans the starting point for the ethical advice is Paul's discussion of the Jew/Greek problem, though it would not be correct to see this as its basis.

The reason for writing Philemon determines the advice offered. It has to do only with one issue, the fate of Onesimus, a runaway slave, whom Paul has been instrumental in converting while in bonds. Philemon should receive him back as if he were Paul (Philemon 17)—not as a slave, but as a brother (v. 16).

In both Colossians and Ephesians, Paul's approach takes on cosmic dimensions, though the same earthbound issues still appear. Because of the polemical context of Colossians one earlier piece of advice is turned on its ear: no one is to judge Christians (Col. 2:16–23). A catalog of sins (3:5–11) and of virtues (3:12–17) precedes a discussion of wives and husbands, children and fathers, slaves and masters (3:18 to 4:1). The principle of mutuality is not applied as thoroughly as in Corinthians. Instead, the relationships are treated in a slightly imbalanced way. In both, Paul is much more careful and less direct, for he is dealing with a congregation he does not know. The context for his discussion is his conviction that Jesus Christ—and Christians—are in a cosmic struggle.

Of all his other letters only Galatians and, to a lesser **extent,** Romans deal explicitly with the question of behav**ioral** freedom. Neither does so in the light of a radical assertion of freedom. But each letter does, in its own way, contribute to a fuller understanding of the basis and scope of Paul's ethics. Implicitly the question of freedom underlies all of Paul's paraenetic advice. He is always faced either with the problem of those who wish to infringe his or others' freedom, or with the problem of those who wish to intimidate others by their assertion of freedom. To the one group he asserts his right to be all things to all men, to the other he proclaims that not everything is helpful.

7. Conclusion

It remains true that the main challenge to Paul in his own churches comes from the left. In some instances, if not in all, the opposition is pushing known Pauline positions too far for Paul's liking and for the good of the congregation. Complicating this picture is the fact that the interpretation of Paul's view by his churches has become more radical through the influence of other important factors: radical Hellenistic Judaism, proto-gnosticizing tendencies, and Greek philosophical speculation. In response to this Paul argues on their ground (which may be simply his own ground) that everything is lawful, but certain limits must be established—most notably the limits of helpfulness for oneself and care for the well-being of others.

The overriding criterion for all behavior is love, a love that indicates the Spirit's presence. Love is his best gift, transcending all other *charismata.* When the *charismata* are exercised, there must be a proper concern for the whole community of believers. Such a concern is fundamental to ethical decisions as well. Only if one has a proper view of the church as the body of Christ, will one be motivated toward the right kinds of behavior.

A secondary challenge to Paul comes from the right. Though not limited to the Palestinian churches, the spiritual home of this opposition is the church of Jerusalem. The distance between Paul and the leaders of the Jerusalem church is not as great as is sometimes imagined, at least not in matters of Christology and mission. There is likely to be a bigger difference in ethics, giving rise to suspicions about Paul's attitudes.

In the face of this Paul asserts that he can be all things to all men. He extends this principle to include those within his churches, though that assertion of freedom is not stated very often. Nevertheless, it is apparent from Paul's own behavior that this is an important part of Paul's ethic, and one that we know of only because of his more conservative brethren.

VI

Weakness and Strength

ALL WAS NOT sweetness and light in early Christianity. While there was a fresh and demonstrable new life—shown in love and joy and peace and other fruits of the Spirit—there was also a good bit of distress, friction, and antagonism. Had there not been the demonstration of the Spirit, the struggling church would not have grown. Had there not been friction, we would know far less about the church, for it is through the friction that we get our most transparent glimpses of the church. We see the church attempting to work out its difficulties in the material that is now available to us in Paul's letters. For this, we should be grateful.

Paul's ethical stance has already been investigated in some detail, concentrating mostly on I and II Corinthians and the views of freedom expressed in that correspondence. It is obvious that Paul was not immune from attack; indeed, on occasion he invited it. As an apostle he was exposed, open to attack from right and from left, from conservatives and from radicals. In turn he attacked them, seeking to demonstrate the adequacy and cogency of *his* understanding of the good news about Jesus. In doing so, he was also implicitly supporting those who were relatively defenseless.

When faced with conflicts, Paul found the strong/weak metaphor particularly appropriate. But because each situation was fluid he applied the metaphor in constantly fluctuating ways. It can be traced through his letters chronologically: I Corinthians, II Corinthians, Romans, and Ephesians, in each case with different emphases. But why was the metaphor appropriate? And why did it change? In his churches Paul was faced with a mixed constituency. Converts to belief in Jesus as the Messiah had come from a variety of backgrounds. Some had been Jews, some had been Gentiles. Some of the latter had already become proselytes before becoming Christians. People with previously pagan convictions stood side by side with those from a conservative Jewish background (see Chapter I).

1. I Corinthians

A major factor in the problems being faced in Corinth was the presence of a radical group of Christians who adopted a "superior" view of their brand of Christianity and put down those who had a simpler view. Their superiority was based on knowledge, wisdom, and a spiritual perception of the world. Another group were foot draggers, somewhat more conservative and certainly more timid. Not only did they not accept the others' view of knowledge, they rejected the libertarian principles of the others and they may not have had the more dramatic spiritual gifts.

Paul countered the extreme claims the radical group made, though he accepted some of their arguments. The one thing he did not tolerate, apart from their undercutting of the significance of Jesus' death and resurrection, was their superior attitude toward others. Paul's concern in such a circumstance was for the weak, those who were uncertain, fearful of the implications of their reception of the good news. They worried over their ability to live up to the level of the superior ones—the strong.

In I Corinthians the strong/weak contrast is not particularly highly developed and does not always have the same
force. It occurs in I Cor., ch. 8, in the midst of Paul's discussion of eating food offered to idols. Not everyone can fully
accept that an idol has no existence (I Cor. 8:7, 4); some who
eat this food which has been dedicated to a god think they
are really continuing to participate in the worship of the idol.
This is an easily understandable attitude, especially among
recent converts. Paul describes them as "weak" persons (vs.
9, 11) with "weak" consciences (vs. 7, 10, 12). The term
"strong" is not used here at all.

The persons with weak consciences are trying to live as
Christians, fighting off the old ways that had characterized
them when they actually worshiped idols. They are struggling to be consistent, but their attempt is being jeopardized
by those who have come farther and faster in the Christian
life. For the strong (if we may call them that) the scruples of
the weak are trivial. "Knowledge" shows them that idols do
not exist, and that therefore idol food has no significance, so
one can eat as one wishes. The weak, much as they might
wish to believe that, cannot. The danger is the emotional
connection between one's past and present. They carry too
much baggage along with them. To avoid placing stumbling
blocks in the way of the weak, Paul counsels not to eat this
food.

This same attitude is repeated in Paul's statement of his
principles of accommodation in I Cor. 9:22: "To the weak I
became weak, that I might win the weak." This paragraph,
I Cor. 9:19–23, is one of the most important indications of
Paul's *own* ethical position. He sets out his own practice in
clear and unequivocal terms, indicating the range of behav-
iors that characterize his own life. His conclusion in v. 22, "I
have become all things to all men, so that I might in every
way win some," summarizes his freedom to adapt his own

response to situations, and it states again—what was stated at each stage of his description—his purpose in all this: to win some.

The ethical position that Paul describes as his own in I Cor. 9:19ff. is extended to include others in I Cor. 10:31 to 11:1. There he states that his willingness to adapt should be followed by others (cf. 11:1, "Be imitators of me, as I am of Christ").

Just prior to this, he discusses idol food again. In I Cor. 10:23ff. he repeats the Corinthians' slogan "All things are lawful," then modifies it by two emphatic "buts"—not all things are helpful and not all things build up (10:23). What is important is the "good of one's neighbor" (10:24). So one can "eat whatever is sold in the meat market without raising questions on the ground of conscience" (10:25), unless someone else raises the problem. Then one should defer (8:13; cf. 10:28–29) so that another's weak conscience will not be offended, for another's conscience must not be destroyed. However, since the whole earth is the Lord's (10:26), Christians are free to eat whatever they like, even at a dinner party hosted by an unbeliever (10:27).

At this point there is a surprise and perhaps some degree of inconsistency. Paul says one should not allow one's own liberty to be determined by another's scruples (I Cor. 10:29b). It is likely that vs. 28–29a should be bracketed, so that v. 29b follows v. 27. It seems that weak Christians were using their weakness aggressively, to keep others from doing things that offended them. We all know Christians who have tried to force their scruples on others as checks to the exercise of another's freedom. This is illegitimate. While there is a genuine weak conscience which must be considered carefully, there is also a correct sense in which the weak should not be given deference. And that is a very fine line.

Later, while describing his view of the unity and mutuality

of the body, Paul makes it perfectly clear that even those with weaker consciences are indispensable parts of the body (I Cor. 12:22). Not only do the weak have their part to play, Paul seems to believe that all Christians are weak (15:43). Only the future risen body will be a "strong" one.

The weak/strong contrast is found also in I Cor. 1:25–27. Here, though, Paul's point is different; he wishes to demolish the arguments of those who are urging "wisdom" as the answer to everything. According to the world's standards, the Corinthians are not a very wise or powerful group. God chose them precisely so that his way would stand out against the way of the world. He shames the world's standards of wisdom and strength by choosing those whom the world considers foolish and weak. In this way not only can no one boast (1:27–31), but God's own foolishness and weakness are shown to be wiser and stronger than men (1:25). Later Paul will develop this idea further.

Paul appears to associate himself with the weak, both in I Cor. 4:10 and in II Cor., chs. 10 to 13. He does so not because he views himself as having a weak conscience but because he is viewed with the same disdain by those who are filled with knowledge, the ones who think they are already reigning (I Cor. 4:8). These "superior" Christians imagine that the Kingdom is here and that they are a part of the reign of God. Here he *does* refer to them as "strong," as over against the apostles, who are weak; they are "wise" in Christ, but he is a fool for Christ; they are held in honor, he in disrepute. His association with the weak is not so much a similarity of outlook, but a similarity in the way he and they are treated by the radical group in Corinth.

2. II CORINTHIANS

Every instance of the strong/weak language in II Corinthians comes in chs. 10 to 13, that section in which Paul defends his apostleship and polemicizes against others who also claim apostolic status. The main feature of the strong/weak contrast in these chapters is that God uses weakness as a way of demonstrating his own power. This is an expansion of Paul's view in I Cor. 1:25–27, applied to Paul himself as an apostle. So he views himself as meek and gentle and humble (II Cor. 10:1) but filled with divine power for destroying strongholds (10:4; we can hardly avoid the conclusion that these strongholds are the constructions of the radicals as in 10:5–6). He is accused of being weak when present, but weighty and strong by letter (10:10). As in I Cor. 1:25–27, the strong/weak contrast is closely connected with the wise/foolish one; the Corinthians are wise, they regard Paul as a fool (II Cor. 11:16ff.). He views himself as weak (11:21), but in this weakness he identifies with the weak in the churches for which he cares (11:28), becoming indignant over their ill-treatment by those who make them fall. All his troubles further serve to underline his weakness (11:21–27), but it is precisely in these things that he boasts (11:30; 12:5).

Now Paul plays a trump card. His own physical weakness (II Cor. 12:7) reminds him of a special revelation from the Lord, who said, "My grace is enough for you; power finds its full strength in weakness" (12:9). It is precisely in Paul's weakness that Christ's power can be made evident (12:9), so that, when he is weak, he is really strong (12:10). Paul obviously feels deeply about this, for he contrasts his "nothingness" with the apostles' superiority (12:11ff.). Later he heightens this contrast by referring to Christ's weakness when crucified but his power when raised from the dead

(13:3–4). Similarly, he is weak in Christ but he participates with Christ in his risen power. Nevertheless he is glad when he is weak if it will result in the Corinthians being genuinely strong (13:9), improving and holding to the faith (13:5).

In brief, the Corinthian correspondence illuminates three aspects of the strong/weak contrast. *(a)* Some Christians have weak consciences about eating customs, as a result of past commitments to idols. Paul is deeply concerned that the struggle for freedom in the Corinthian church not destroy them. *(b)* Paul identifies himself as weak over against the pillar apostles. This weakness has two sides to it: he is physically weak and so can be looked down on, but because he is weak he depends even more on the power of Christ. As a result, Christ's power is more apparent in Paul than in the others. *(c)* The gospel itself is "weak," in the sense that it is foolish and despised. But thereby God's power is even more evident, for he uses weakness to shame strength, foolishness to shame wisdom.

3. ROMANS

The section in Romans from 12:1 through 15:33 offers ethical advice to the Roman church. Some of it is parallel to the instructions given in I Corinthians, but phrased more openly and generally as one would expect in a letter addressed to a church that Paul neither founded nor knew. The letter was probably written about the same time as II Cor., chs. 10 to 13, and therefore provides a useful comparison.

Paul has some knowledge of problems in Rome. From Rom., ch. 11, we may surmise that there is tension between Jewish and Gentile Christians over their respective places in God's scheme of things (Rom. 11:17, 20, 22, 25). Gentiles are boasting of their importance and lording it over their Jewish fellow believers who preceded them in belief in Jesus. This is intolerable, and Paul attempts to state a more satisfactory view in ch. 11.

In Rom., ch. 14, where the strong/weak language surfaces, it is likely that the Jew/Gentile issue is still in the background. The dominant theme in ch. 14 is that one is not to judge another's behavior (Rom. 14:3, 4, 10, 13, 22). Instead, one is to build up the other (14:19) and avoid laying stumbling blocks (14:13). One is to please the neighbor for the neighbor's good (15:1–2) so that the whole congregation may together glorify God (15:6). The problems in this congregation overlap with the Corinthian problems: diet (14:1–4, 14–23), observances (14:5–9), and the relationship of Jew and Gentile (15:7–13).

With respect to diet, one important difference from I Corinthians may be noted: there is no reference to idol food. Whether because the situation is different or the problem is not clear, Paul's advice is generalized. Both opinions are acceptable (Rom. 14:1–4); one may eat a full menu, or only a vegetable diet. Paul's own opinion, however, is that any food is acceptable (14:14). Nevertheless, food is not so important as a person's standing before God, so the primary concern is not to destroy someone else through one's actions.

The question about the observance of days is encountered only here and later in Colossians. Paul does not really care very much about the rights and wrongs of the different positions being adopted. He cares only for the relationships that are affected by this disagreement. The basic principle, as in the previous example, is that each is to be fully convinced in his own mind (Rom. 14:5; cf. 14:23). Paul in fact explicitly connects the two questions in 14:6; in both cases he is quite prepared to grant the legitimacy of each group's motives (both do it in honor of the Lord) and the adequacy of their argument.

The third question has to do with Jew and Gentile relationships, suggesting that in Rome the strong/weak problems are created by the tension between Christian Jews and Christian Gentiles. It seems from Rom. 15:7–13 that the two groups (if they be groups) are no longer accepting each other. Paul believes, on the basis of the information available to him, that it is the Gentile Christians who are posing the problem. He points out to them that Christ became a servant to the circumcision so that the Gentiles might ultimately glorify God (15:8–9). In several of the quotations from the Old Testament Scriptures cited by Paul the central idea is the inclusion of the Gentiles with Israel. This is particularly evident in Rom. 15:10 in the quotation from Deut. 32:43 ("Rejoice, Gentiles, with his people"); in the quotation of Ps. 117:1 (in Rom. 15:11); and in the quotation of Isa. 11:10 (in Rom. 15:12). Though these are capable of the opposite interpretation (that the problem arises because the Christian Jews are cutting off the Gentiles), the interpretation that the problems originate with the Gentiles is reinforced by two factors.

The first of these is the implication of Rom., ch. 11, to which reference has already been made. The second is the different character of the problems in Rome from those in I Corinthians. The food problem does not arise from idol meat, as one would expect if Gentiles were "weak," but involves a vegetarian approach that has been coupled with the observance of special days. When phrased this way, it sounds as if Jewish Christians are attempting to defend their scruples over *kosher* meat and the festivals. Paul sides with the views of the Gentile Christians that these are not necessary, but, consistent with I Corinthians, he sides with the underdog— the weak—in his practice.

Why is this question important? If this interpretation is correct, we have here an extremely significant indication of a newly developing problem in the practice of freedom in the early church. In Galatians, for example, a crucial problem arises out of different perceptions of the gospel's effect on Christian freedom. The questions are whether a Gentile Christian must be circumcised and whether he will have to keep the law. In Galatians, Paul responds by saying, "Don't succumb for a moment!" Both questions have receded in I and II Corinthians and Romans.

In Romans an issue involving the observance of special days and vegetarian practices surfaces in a discussion about Jew and Gentile. Paul's attitude is that it does not matter. Let everyone do what seems right. Only, don't put a stumbling block in another person's way. This attitude is quite foreign to the view adopted in Galatians.

Why? The answer is to be found in the way Paul views the limitation on one's freedom. Freedom is essential, but it is always to be exercised in a way that will not destroy others. In Galatians the Gentile Christians were in danger, in Romans it is the Jewish Christians. Both need to be protected, but the conditions are so different that a new approach needs to be taken in each situation.

Circumstances are altering in the church. Freedom continues to be a problem, but it is no longer a problem between left-wing and right-wing Jews nor between radicals and the weak. It now involves Gentile Christians and Jewish Christians. The latter are in danger of being coerced by the Gentile Christians. Those who should be strong, who should have a full understanding of the purposes of God, who should know what God is doing, who should be able to lead the Gentiles to faith are being viewed as weak in the faith. And the Gentiles, who are Johnny-come-latelies and therefore might be expected to be weak, are the "strong" ones.

One last comment. In Romans, Paul identifies himself as one of the "strong" (15:1). In I Corinthians he needed to argue in a different way and called himself "weak." Here he sides with the strong and uses himself as an example of a proper balance between adopting "strong" principles and a practice that would avoid making a brother stumble (cf. also I Cor. 9:22).

4. EPHESIANS

To finish this sketch, we may refer to Eph., ch. 2, and then to ch. 6, where two different aspects of this picture are reinforced, and a new one introduced.

There is first of all a reinforcing of the idea that the Gentiles are now assuming a dominant role in the church. A consideration of the Gentiles is begun in Eph. 2:11ff. which starts from the idea that they are distant from God's blessing but asserts that they have been brought near through Christ and have become one with the Jews through the breaking down of the dividing wall of hostility. So Gentiles are no longer outlanders (2:19ff.) but fellow citizens. This demonstrates how the earlier expectation for Jewish salvation, expressed so fully in Romans, comes to be overlooked only a few years later. Here there is no sense of expectation, only an expression of how totally Gentiles are integrated. I am inclined to think that, as time went on, Jews were considered to be the weak ones within the church. In Romans that was implicit in the way the problem was discussed. In Ephesians it seems simply assumed.

The second point emphasized in Ephesians is the power of God. In closing this letter in 6:10–20, though the word "weak" is never used, Paul does talk about strength. But now it is a strength that applies to everyone, not a strong group as opposed to a weak group. The strength that is needed is needed by the church *as a whole* in its fight against the devil and all his cosmic manifestations—principalities, powers, world rulers of this age, spiritual powers of evil even in heavenly places (Eph. 6:11–12). This can obviously be connected with his earlier expressions of the need for God's power (as in II Cor., ch. 13, particularly), but here that idea has been greatly extended and the struggle has been lifted to a totally different plane—to the cosmic dimension.

The third point to note in Ephesians is a new one. All the earlier indications of church-related concerns have come to fruition. In Ephesians, as in Colossians, the church is viewed not just as a local group but as a single universal organism, cosmic in its scope. Thus the church is likened to the temple of the Lord, a dwelling place of the Spirit (Eph. 2:19–22). These ideas are developed out of, but different from, the earlier descriptions. A concern for the church has generally been present in Paul, but is here much more fully presented. It controls his whole presentation. It may be that the absence of explicit references to freedom in both Colossians and Ephesians is related to this. There are two reasons for saying this. In the early heady days of charismatic experience, there can be an awareness of the Spirit and of freedom that is intense. As time goes on, that can fade. This seems to have been the case in early Christianity where so many problems attended the early experiences of the freedom of the Spirit. The second reason for saying this is that a universal church idea carries with it, for Paul, an increasing sense of order and stability (see, for example, the hesitation on the ethical questions in 5:21 to 6:9; the slightly altered view of the body in 4:4–16; the more developed notion of Christ as the head in v.15; and so on). This in turn contributes to the notion of a universal church with a universal set of standards. There is less room for local differences and for internal struggles. Freedom is less often sought and less frequently expressed. The enthusiasm of the forties and fifties gives way to the steady building of the sixties.

In summary, Ephesians witnesses to the universalizing of the earlier solutions. They have been taken out of the realm of specific questions in specific church settings, and have been generalized, spiritualized, and made cosmic in scope. The Gentile ascendancy in the church is more apparent, the problems created by Jew/Greek tensions seem to have faded, and the problem of freedom is never raised.

5. CONCLUSION

In the four letters surveyed briefly here we find four different stages with respect to the strong/weak question. In some respects this development is characteristic of the church—or at least the Pauline churches—as a whole.

In I Corinthians the immediate problems are local and specific. How should the strong treat those whose consciences are weaker? That answer is to defer in matters of behavior, but not principle, to the weak. God himself acts in an analogous way. Though he is strong, he uses weak things to show his power.

In II Corinthians, Paul goes beyond siding with the weak to identify himself as weak. He argues that his being weak is one way in which God can make fuller use of him, for God's strength is then essential if Paul's ministry is to bear any fruit at all. One can hardly avoid the corollary that the "superlative" apostles are relying on their own strength.

In Romans the strong/weak problems are not related to freedom, as in I Corinthians, nor to apostolic questions, as in II Corinthians, but to Jew/Gentile problems. The difficulty is not the assertion of one's right to freedom but the assertion of a limitation: "One must not, because. . . ." In this Paul sides with those who see new things in store, but he cautions them not to judge the Jewish Christians.

In Ephesians the whole freedom context is left behind for a church-centered view of the strength of God. Paul arms the *church* for its cosmic struggle, and gives generalized, but more cautious, ethical advice.

In the changing application of the strong/weak metaphor certain important principles emerge. These he treats as the more important questions, in preference to laying down firm advice on some of the specific questions at issue. Some of these may be put in capsule form.

a. Give way to others. This is a basic principle for Paul in situations where giving way will not endanger the gospel or mislead some into misconceiving the nature of Christ's redemption.

b. Don't give way to others. This is an obvious principle when the core of the gospel is at stake. But it also applies in circumstances where someone who is strong (or should be strong) is attempting to force his scruples on a weaker Christian and is holding him up to ethical blackmail. In such circumstances, don't give way.

c. Behavior changes according to need. This principle takes seriously the varying demands of the good news as it confronts different people: Jews, Greeks; male, female; law-bound, law-free; etc. The attitude one takes and the behavior one adopts will depend upon whether the other is being viewed as strong or as weak.

d. Weakness can be strength. It is not a weakness to be weak, nor is it always a strength to be strong. God redeems one's own weakness by making use of it to demonstrate his own strength.

e. Don't judge another. This is a negative implication of all the preceding, and it goes hand in hand with the following positive principle.

f. Build up the other. A proper concern focuses not just on the gospel and on one's own behavior, but it properly focuses on the other's need. His good is to be served. He should never be destroyed, always built up.

g. Finally, God's strength is cosmic. The Christian who allows God's power to be demonstrated in him or her shares in the cosmic dimensions of that strength.

On the basis of such principles Paul worked away at the problems the strong and the weak presented to him in his congregations. He recognized the range of possible courses of action and encouraged considerable freedom in the resolution of those problems. Neither the strong nor the weak were always right.

Out of his consideration of these questions, Paul developed a larger view of the resources that God has available for his people. Where one is willing to admit weakness, especially in the face of the great cosmic struggles, God will provide strength. So the weak must never be despised, for they will be a surer sign of God's power than the strong.

It is by now obvious that the church is continuing to grow and develop. The issues the church faces change. Whereas earlier Paul had to deal straightforwardly with problems of freedom and license and conservatism and timidity, later he has to deal with a church largely Gentile in its makeup as it begins to develop new structures and institutions, as it seeks to confront an increasingly hostile Gentile world with its mythical world views. These kinds of changes require new responses. Paul is nothing if not adaptable and creative. Toward the end of his life he develops yet more insights into the purpose and power of God.

The church often makes use of the vocabulary "weak" and "strong," especially the notion of the weaker brother. It is often overlooked that the one who is weak, in the New Testament use of the word, is precisely the one who should be strong. And for Paul, the one who claims to be strong is often in fact weak. It would be interesting to speculate on the effect of applying this reversal of categories in our setting. Is it

possible that sometimes those who seem to know what everyone else should do are in fact weaker brothers? Is it possible
that the one who seems extremely vulnerable is in fact more
likely to know the supporting power of God?

Whatever the result of such speculation, it is obvious that
for Paul the church is the place where these issues are to be
worked out. The church does not figure too largely in Paul's
early writings; it comes increasingly to dominate his thought.
To this more institutional concern we now turn.

VII

Order and Charisma

A GROWING CONSCIOUSNESS of the church as an institution brings with it an increasing concern for church order and a reduced interest in freedom. In this chapter we shall ask about freedom in the church, Paul's understanding of a collective expression of freedom, the stress on *charisma,* and the inability of these emphases to survive.

1. THE NEED FOR ORDER

Both Colossians and Ephesians show a lively concern for the church and its well-being. In both, "church" means not the local church (as it does in almost every case in the earlier letters where the plural "churches" is normal usage) but rather the "universal church." Though this is not a Pauline phrase, it is a necessary paraphrase for conveying the later meaning of the word "church."

As he moves toward a concern for the church in its totality Paul continues to express an interest in the way the church's ministry is arranged. Indeed, in I and II Timothy and Titus, which we have left out of consideration, the concern for ministry takes up a disproportionate amount of space. Whether these are Pauline or not, they demonstrate a growing concern for questions of order, stability, transmission of authority, correctness, purity. In this respect the young church has come full circle. It has returned to a large degree to its Jewish roots, with the sense of stability, order, and authority. A more extensive study of church developments in the first and early second centuries would show that many of the institutions of the early church were based on Jewish practices. Models are helpful, and Judaism is the most obvious and adequate source. These developments in the later parts of the Pauline collection provide a contrast to the situation described in the earlier letters. The contrast should not be exaggerated, but it is real and pervasive.

For example, this difference can be seen by comparing quickly the lists of ministerial functions in I Corinthians, Romans, and Ephesians. Each has overlapping lists of *charismata* (spiritual gifts) and functions in the church. But, though the variations are noteworthy, it is in their assumptions that they differ most notably. In I Cor. 12:4–31 (even its length is remarkable) the assumption is expressly stated that *each* is given a manifestation of the Spirit (12:7, 11) so that the body may be properly diverse (12:14ff.) and adequately able to care for the various parts, whether "weak" or "honorable" (12:22–26). The controlling assumption is that the Spirit offers gifts to everyone in the church.

In Rom. 12:1–7 some of these same ideas are present, but in a more muted way. The stress is not on the gifts of the Spirit but on dedication of oneself to God (Rom. 12:1-2). The church is the body, individually Christians are members of it, and each has a function that differs according to God's grace (12:4–6). There is, however, no mention of the Spirit; only of the *charismata*.

Later, in Colossians, the Son is described as the *head* of the body (Col. 1:18; see also Eph. 1:22–23), a new idea completely. In Eph., ch. 4, the church is no longer simply the body of Christ, but Christ's headship is the whole point of the metaphor (4:15–16). With respect to ministry in the church (4:1–16) the gifts described are for "each of us" (4:7), yet only some within the congregation seem to be included (4:11). Over against those who have gifts are the "saints," who are to be built up into the body (4:12). Though reference is made to the Spirit (4:3), he does not give gifts, he creates unity in the body since there is one hope, one Lord, one faith, one baptism, one God and Father.

This brief comparison of one idea demonstrates that there are important differences in the Pauline letters. To anticipate the conclusion, we may state at the outset that there are four basic stages in this development.

a. The first stage includes Galatians, and I and II Thessalonians. There is little or no concern for the ordering of the church or for the gifts exercised in the church. The end is near. There are enough things to worry about without worrying over institutional concerns.

b. The second stage includes I and II Corinthians, Romans, and Philippians. This stage is marked by a considerable concern for gifts, but little concern for order. The church is described in dynamic terms. What matters is that each member has an opportunity to use the gifts that are given.

c. The third stage reverses these concerns, so that the question of order begins to take the larger role and the matter of gifts a smaller role. The two are still held in balance, but the balance has changed.

d. The fourth stage is a post- or non-Pauline one in which gifts are viewed in a truncated way; they are available basically only to a "ministerial group" and order is a dominant problem.

Such a schematization could be misleading if pressed too far. It does pose starkly, however, the nature of the problem facing the early church: how to relate the enthusiasm found in the Spirit with the need for order in the exercise of the Spirit's gifts? The standard response has always been a quotation from Paul: Let all things be done decently and in order (I Cor. 14:40). That advice offered to the church at Corinth was necessary precisely because there was no order. And so the questions become: How and why was it unorderly? What did Paul recommend to try to make it more orderly? And what happened then? To try to answer these questions, we will have to rely upon I Corinthians once again.

2. STAGE ONE

In Galatians, and in I and II Thessalonians, there is very little that bears directly on the question of *charisma* and order. Helpful information about Paul's view of apostleship and of the need for authority would be available for a more extensive study than this. But on the role of individual Christians and their interrelationships there is nothing. Paul's extensive treatment of freedom in Galatians contains no corresponding advice about the exercise of freedom in the church. We learn only that no one is to envy another (Gal. 5:26); instead, each is to bear others' burdens (6:2). Likewise in I Thessalonians one can assume that there is some notion of authority in the church ("Respect those who labor among you and are over you in the Lord," I Thess. 5:12), but nothing more about the exercise of gifts. The organization of the church and the nature of the relationships within it have no chance to show through.

It is difficult to escape two negative conclusions. First, at this early stage in Paul's correspondence (A.D. 48–50) there is no pressing need to develop a theoretical or theological basis for gifts of the Spirit and their exercise in the church. It would appear that the *charismata,* if they are being exercised at all (and I am confident they are; cf. Gal. 3:2, 5), are not posing any problem. Further, the church need not be viewed as a permanent institution destined for a long future. The time is short. The end is near. Jesus is coming. Do what needs to be done, and do it as quickly as possible. Experience whatever can be experienced of the Spirit. Use his gifts in whatever way is useful.

The second conclusion must be that there is almost no evidence of a legacy from Jesus about the church's structure or activities. The group called the Twelve has almost entirely dropped from sight; there is only a slight awareness that it is the foundation of the church. No inherited institutions or assumptions about order, except Baptism and the Lord's Supper, are present in the early Pauline letters, and even the evidence for the latter is extremely tenuous at this stage. This same conviction is reinforced by the early chapters of Acts. A critical assessment of the evidence makes it apparent that Jesus did not lay down any ordering principles for the church. In Acts the church is on its own, conscious of the dynamic presence of the Spirit, trying first of all to discover pragmatic solutions to its immediate problems, such as its need for sharing, common worship, accommodating the widows, and so on.

Positively, the evidence from these three letters and from the early chapters of Acts suggests that the church is coping fairly well with the need to find new ways to develop its bonds in Jesus Christ. The problems are difficult but not devastating. There is a sense of excitement, enthusiasm, and originality. The rather rapid growth of the church probably creates its own special set of difficulties, but these do not assume a primary place. Attention can be focused on other more important questions.

These conclusions confirm the view that during this earliest stage the church is unstructured, unordered, and still feeling its way. It is conscious of living in an intervening period, after Jesus has come and before he returns. The church is simply not concerned with questions of order, though Paul is concerned about the question of authority and his position vis-à-vis the other apostles. This absence of evidence is quite eloquent.

3. STAGE TWO

The second stage includes the great letters—I Corinthians, II Corinthians, Romans, and Philippians. These letters show clearly a better articulated concern for church developments. The church as an entity is much more important than in the earlier letters. What goes on within the local church is vital to its health; as a result, there is considerable discussion of the quality of the relationships between members of the churches. It is striking, for example, that all but three of the references to *charismata* in the New Testament are found in Romans and I and II Corinthians, indicating a focal concern for the gifts of the Spirit at this middle stage.

In these letters we have the first attempts to define the body concept. There is a stress on mutuality, completeness, and individual contributions. There is also clear evidence of problems arising from some being strong and some weak (see Chapter VI), together with a lively concern for the health and well-being of all parts of the church. The church is described in terms that force us to recognize its own attempts to order itself. It recognizes that there is a diversity of gifts, not always clearly related, a diversity of functions, and a kind of enthusiasm that may on occasion be uncontrollable and overly excitable.

a. I Corinthians, ch. 12

The Corinthians have asked Paul about spiritual gifts. His reply, taking three chapters, presupposes that this is a pressing issue that requires careful presentation. One introductory observation provides an interesting indication of Paul's attitude. He is asked about spiritual things (*pneumatika,* 12:1; cf. 14:1), but he replies by discussing gifts (*charismata,* 12:4). The pneumatics, the radicals in Corinth, have used a term that emphasizes the hyperspirituality of their gifts. In framing his reply, Paul makes a comment that criticizes a spurious kind of spirituality which can lead to saying "Jesus be anathema" instead of "Jesus is Lord." So, when he begins his discussion of spiritual things he uses a different word. The word *charismata* is connected with God's graciousness in giving the gifts. It is from the same root as the Greek words for "grace" and "thanks." The gifts are received from God through the Spirit, after Jesus is confessed as Lord. It is no accident that Paul prefers this word to one that has been utilized, sometimes incorrectly, by the radicals.

In his initial description of these gifts he stresses their diversity of distribution and of characteristics. But it is the same Spirit, the same Lord, the same God who distributes a variety of gifts, ministries, and activities to all, for service in the body.

The gifts he enumerates are the word of wisdom, the word of knowledge, faith, healing, miracle activity, prophecy, discernment of spirits, tongues, and interpretation of tongues. Even if this were intended to be a complete list, it would be remarkable. But if, as I believe, it is intended to be merely representative, it is even more surprising. It seems simply Paul's attempt to rhyme off in a hurry those *charismata* which he knows are represented in the Corinthian church.

It should be noted that most of the gifts are highly specialized. They can be carried out only when the Spirit qualifies a person for that activity. These are not the ordinary run-of-the-mill activities, but ecstatic phenomena, some intelligible to us and some not, which are characteristic of certain kinds of religious experience.

This list constitutes, perhaps, the best indication of the collective freedom claimed and experienced in the church at Corinth. Under the influence of ecstatic experiences a wide selection of Christians was freely participating in worship activities. Given the roots of the church within the synagogue, this is startling. Gifts to be used in worship should be exercised, according to the synagogue, only by qualified persons. Some gifts, like prophecy, might not be fully legitimate. But in this church the only qualification necessary is the Spirit who gives them. Such is Christian freedom!

If in fact the Corinthian Christians were exercising a wide range of *charismata,* what kind of group experience was involved? We may infer from I Cor. 11:5 that women participated in at least the prophetic gift, and it may be that the reference to praying in vs. 5 and 13 indicates a broader charismatic activity (see Chapter III). So we must reckon it likely that in Corinth the whole Christian community, both men and women, was taking part in the meetings for worship. But some persons may have been vying to outdo others in the dramatic character of these manifestations of the Spirit. Such a possibility is likely when we recall that the chapter on love (I Cor., ch. 13) both exalts love as the more excellent way than all these gifts and engages in a polemic with those who claim that particularly dramatic gifts are the best way.

This claimed superiority emerges also in the body metaphor in I Cor. 12:14–26, where Paul specifically mentions the "weaker parts of the body" (12:22) and the "less honorable parts" (12:23). The major purpose of the body metaphor, coming as it does after the list of *charismata,* is to assert unequivocally that one can no more grade the *charismata* than one can grade the parts of the body. To have a whole body you need all the parts. If only *one* gift were to be found in the church, it would not be a body (12:14ff.). Like a physical body, this body suffers in all its parts if one part is harmed (12:25–26).

So far, then, Paul has stressed the charismatic side of the church's existence. It is constituted as a God-ordained body by the diversity of its parts and of its *charismata.* The church must be a charismatic church with the *charismata* fully integrated into one organism so that each gift assumes its rightful place alongside all the others. When that happens, freedom will exist for the exercise of all gifts.

With I Cor. 12:27 the emphasis, though not the image, changes. Paul still assumes the corporateness of the body and individual participation in that body, but he now provides a hierarchically ordered list. The word "functions" might be helpful to distinguish these from the *charismata,* though Paul does use that word too in 12:28, 30, 31. He repeats some of the former *charismata,* but he seems to be thinking more of the person who exercises that gift than of the gift itself.

The hierarchical structure is apparent from the "first . . . second . . . third . . . then . . . then . . ." arrangement. This second list includes apostles, prophets, teachers, miracle workers, gifts of healing, helpers, leaders, tongues, and, after a series of rhetorical questions, interpretation. These overlapping lists in the same chapter pose problems to which there is no easy answer. It may be that Paul's earlier list did not include any reference to the major authority figures in the primitive church, among whom he counted himself. When he draws up another list he thus repeats some of the *charismata* from his earlier list, but he starts off with a reference to the apostles and other church-building functions. His second list, then, is an attempt to turn the criticism of himself as an apostle and church builder. If the opposition to him in Corinth was, to a large extent, coming from those who claimed dramatic *charismata* high up the earlier list, his use of first, second, etc., in the second list would be doubly useful. By it he asserts the primacy, and probably the unrepeatability, of his *charisma* as an apostle.

Paul indisputably numbered himself among the apostles. Equally indisputably, Paul viewed the apostles as persons with authority in the church. The claim to authority does not rest simply on the historical relationship with Jesus that the Twelve might claim, for the apostles form a group distinct from the Twelve though overlapping with it (I Cor. 15:5, 7). Paul includes Peter and John, who are of the Twelve, as apostles, and also James the Lord's brother, who was not one of the Twelve (cf. Gal. 1:18f.; 2:9). He includes others too in the group of apostles. It is only later that the term "apostles" comes to be used of the Twelve. The process may be seen as it occurs when Mark 3:14 is compared with Matt. 10:2 and Luke 6:13. Apostolic authority, as distinct from the authority of the Twelve, is related both to its origins (seeing the risen Jesus) and to its church-building function (an apostle exercises authority over the churches he plants).

By constructing his second list as he does, Paul is already qualifying his statement about the church as body by claiming apostolic primacy within that body. That same sense is reinforced slightly by his rhetorical questions: "Are all apostles? Are all prophets?" etc. (I Cor. 12:29–30). That too suggests an ordered sequence of gifts to which one might aspire.

Even that is further modified by I Cor. 12:31, where Paul urges the Corinthians to be deeply concerned for the better gifts. One might expect, on the basis of everything he has just said, that these will be apostleship, or prophecy, or teaching. Instead, the whole pattern of the argument is broken; the outstanding way is love. As we have already seen (Chapter V, section 5), love is that gift which above all will continue beyond the end (13:8, 13), so it is the one thing to be pursued (14:1).

Putting all these observations together, we may conclude that Paul's view of the church at this stage is organic. The church is a body that is integrated in all its parts, none of which is superior to the rest. Some might have unique functions because of their special relationship to the risen Jesus, but no matter how special some of these might be, all should pursue love as the one enduring *charisma*. The pursuit of love, however, does not mean that everyone becomes alike. Each is still distinct from the rest in the gifts given; each gift is to be expressed within the integrated body. The church is a charismatic group, inspired by the Spirit who organizes it so that it all fits together. But when all is said and done, Paul never satisfactorily resolves the tension between his two lists of *charismata* and the relationship between the functions of the apostles, prophets, etc., and the rest of the body.

b. I Corinthians, ch. 14

In ch. 14, Paul continues his discussion of charismatic gifts or, as he once again calls them, spiritual gifts (*pneumatika,* 14:1). This time he considers the legitimate limitations on their exercise.

He begins by recommending both love and prophesying and discounting the equally charismatic speaking in tongues (I Cor. 14:1–2). It is apparent in what follows that Paul is on dangerous ground. He knows, and tells the Corinthians, that he himself regularly uses ecstatic speech ("more than you all"), but he limits the use of this gift within the church so that others may be instructed (14:18–19). This autobiographical statement is the key to the whole issue. One should seek all the *charismata* that God offers but should use them wisely and intelligently for building others up, not for exalting one-self. This is the most basic limitation on the exercise of spiritual gifts. Such a view presupposes that the unlimited use of ecstatic or charismatic gifts may tend to disorder. Disorder is not to be allowed and certainly not sought after.

The problem, it is clear, is not with the gifts themselves, nor with their origin in the Spirit, but with the much more mundane features of community life. The gifts do not create disorder, the persons who exercise the gifts do. The problem then is not what the gifts do to the people, but what the people do with the gifts.

Paul believes that speaking in tongues is a way of speaking to God, even though no one else can understand (I Cor. 14:2). He who speaks in tongues is speaking indistinctly (14:6–8), like a foreigner whose language is not understood by others (14:9–11). On the other hand, prophecy is an intelligible activity and is extremely useful, according to Paul, for building the church (14:3–5). The real function of prophecy, in Paul's view, is not a looking into the future, as our popular understanding would have it, but the much more comprehensive role of the Hebrew prophets who addressed themselves to their immediate social and religious and political situation. Prophecy includes encouragement and consolation (14:3), edification (14:4, 5, 12), instruction (14:19), conviction and repentance (14:24–25). Prophecy is, for Paul, the second most important function of the church, ranking between the functions of apostles and teachers (12:27–29), both of which are also edifying and church-building.

Since Paul recognizes that the community is crucially important, more important than the welfare of individual Christians, he values communal activities such as prophecy more highly. When he says that he speaks in tongues more than anyone else, but in church he would rather speak five words intelligibly, he expresses this tension between the private and the community exercise of gifts. The community, because it is collectively the body of Christ, should be a place where a concern for each other (see Chapters IV–VI) animates adequate worship practices that will build up the body. Only what contributes to the well-being of all, and what contributes to the redemption of other nonbelievers, is to be utilized (see I Cor. 14:23–25, and below).

However, speaking in tongues is not just a private activity. It may be used in the community if the Spirit also gives the gift of interpretation (I Cor. 14:13). Paul views tongues as a kind of communion between one's spirit and God (14:14; cf. 14:2; Rom. 8:26), with the activity of the mind apparently left to one side. The mind and the spirit are linked, according to Paul's reasoning, through the interpretation of tongues. The outsider will not have a clue as to what is going on—he cannot say "Amen"—if all speech is ecstatic (14:16–17). Even the insider may be baffled.

This concern is further developed. Paul describes a situation in which unbelievers enter into a Christian meeting where both ecstatic speech and intelligible prophecy are being used. What will their reaction be? There is some difficulty in following Paul's logic, though not his conclusions. He maintains that through prophetic speech unbelievers will be convicted and will recognize the presence of God. Through speaking in tongues, the best they can do is to think Christians are mad (I Cor. 14:23–25).

Now all of this sounds as if Paul has in mind some extensive limitation on the exercise of these *charismata.* That is not really so. He has recommended a limitation of *one* gift, tongues, and even that is a partial limitation. It is qualified by the advice that when one speaks in tongues in the church setting there is to be an interpretation. This view of the Corinthian worship is shown to be correct by I Cor. 14: 26–33. Many of the gifts mentioned in ch. 12 are mentioned

again when Paul describes a typical community gathering,
the only description of its kind in the New Testament. Worship appears much more varied than our hymn, prayer,
hymn, Scripture, hymn, sermon, etc.

There are three essential points to notice: (1) each takes
part when the community gathers (I Cor. 14:26a); (2) the
contribution should aim at edification (14:26b); (3) the gifts
exercised are charismatic (14:26–32). This last point may be
emphasized by listing the expected contributions to the worship of the community: hymns, teachings (perhaps ethical
instruction), revelations, tongues, interpretations, prophecies. In several cases it is anticipated that there will be more
than one contribution.

These activities, though all legitimate in Paul's view, could
tend toward exalting one's own importance or asserting the
preeminence of one's own gift. As a result he suggests countering this in several ways: only two or three should speak in
tongues; those who speak should do so in turn; each ecstatic
utterance needs to be interpreted; when someone prophesies,
others should judge it; when revelations are given, others are
to be silent. Such instructions presuppose that confusion has
taken over under the guise of spiritual experience. Those who
are contributing to the confusion assume that the exercise of
their gift is more important than the exercise of others' gifts.
To such a situation Paul's advice about the body and its many
parts speaks eloquently. If the community is really the community of God's people, and if the gifts are really God's gifts,
the gathering should not be one of confusion at all, for God
does not create confusion but peace (14:33).

The answer to confusion is not to limit arbitrarily either
the gifts or those who are gifted. Whatever God gives, and
to whomever he gives it, will be useful for building up God's
people. The exercise of the *charismata* is the primary matter.
Order is distinctly subordinate, useful only to create a harmo-

nious setting in which the gifts can be used. Since it is not primary, community activities should not be predicated upon order. They can only be built upon what the Spirit gives. God will look after the confusion if the members of the community treat each other with the consideration each deserves.

c. Women

There is one important qualification to all this: the role of women and their gifts (see Chapter III). Paul appears not to allow them to "speak" in church (I Cor. 14:34–35), they are to be silent, subordinate, and to learn at home. This is unexpected for two reasons: first, Paul has already spoken approvingly of women praying and prophesying in ch. 11, and second, he seems to wish everyone in the primitive community to play an appropriate role. Why should not women also have a role to play, especially if they have already demonstrated that they have some of the gifts?

Paul does not require absolute passivity in women. He names women as important ministers of the gospel. The two most important instances are in Rom. 16:1 with reference to Phoebe from Cenchreae and in Rom. 16:3 concerning Priscilla or Prisca (cf. I Cor. 16:19). Further examples are Mary (Rom. 16:6), Tryphaena and Tryphosa (Rom. 16:12), Julia (Rom. 16:15), Nympha (Col. 4:15), and Apphia (Philemon 2). It is difficult to imagine, even for practical reasons emerging from the Corinthian milieu, that Paul really wishes to limit all female participation in worship.

He does not state that women cannot be given gifts. There is no indication that the Lord cannot work among them as well. Though he excludes them from "speaking" in church, it is not certain that he means to exclude all charismatic activities. It may be a much more restricted prohibition which relates in some way to his wish that they should "learn" at home, by "asking" their husbands.

One reconstruction is the following. Paul has previously encouraged women to participate in worship. As a result, the Christian community has developed a new relationship between men and women, so that they are sitting together in the meeting, a practice not allowed in the synagogue. But some persons, probably the radicals or pneumatics, are encouraging too great a participation by women in the meetings. Others oppose this tendency, partly because it is creating misunderstandings on the outside as well. Paul then counsels a limitation on women's participation. That limitation seems on first sight to be all-inclusive, but may not in fact be so. It is more likely a limitation on asking their husbands questions in church, or perhaps a limitation on taking over teaching functions. Whatever it may be, no limit is expressed on the exercise of charismatic gifts. We might well imagine women continuing to exercise their *charismata,* while still obeying the intention of Paul's demand to be silent. On this view the gifts take precedence over the Biblical injunction to be subordinate.

d. Summary of I Corinthians

Before commenting on later developments, we should gather up some strands.

(1) The church is best pictured as a body, needing all its parts to be a real body. Each part, no matter how important or unimportant it might seem, has its own place.

(2) The church's freedom is a function of the exercise of the *charismata,* those gifts of the Spirit which transcend ordinary human qualities, in which each Christian shares. Though all gifts are from the same Spirit, some (the community founding gifts) are more important than others; whatever one's role, everyone should seek the best gift of love.

(3) Within church worship everyone has a part to play.

This part is not assigned or "ordered" but is rather exercised at the free instigation of the Spirit, with the goal of building up the body.

(4) The disorder and confusion of the church in Corinth must be resolved but without limiting the exercise of *all* the gifts.

(5) The role of women is in dispute. Certain activities are acknowledged, but in general their role is downgraded.

e. Other Developments

It is surprising that we can add very little to this picture from II Corinthians. In Romans we find a differently balanced treatment of some of the same questions discussed in I Corinthians, particularly of the body metaphor. The body is still viewed as *one* body in Christ (Rom. 12:4–5) which has numerous members all with different functions. The gifts listed are prophecy, service, teaching, exhortation, contributions, aid, and merciful acts. It is immediately apparent that the gifts in this list are not so dramatic. The reason may be that Paul wants to be cautious in what he says to an unknown church. To list the more dramatic gifts might seem boasting if that church was not actually experiencing all those gifts. Such an assertion of spiritual superiority would be out of place, especially in the light of what he says in Rom., chs. 2 and 11.

4. STAGE THREE

While the description of the body in Romans is not so intense as in I Corinthians, it is basically similar. In the description of the body in Ephesians, while superficially the same, the picture has changed in several important respects. Some of these were referred to at the beginning of this chapter: *(a)* The body idea has been further developed; its head is Christ. It is the Christian's "growing up into the head" that is important, not the mutual dependence of the diverse members. *(b)* The Spirit continues to be important, but not so much for giving gifts as for creating unity. *(c)* The gifts are more limited in scope. *(d)* The recipients seem to be restricted.

It is important to develop these last two ideas further. In Eph. 4:7, Paul says that each Christian has been given a gift. But the gift given to each is not seen as one among a wide variety of gifts, available of necessity for the proper fitting together of the body. The gift is a common gift, "grace," which is given according to the measure of the gift of Christ. This is a crucially important idea for the understanding of the basis of the church. It is not something that establishes a basis, however, for the church's understanding of itself as a corporate fellowship, which is the question under discussion (4:1–7). The starting point for the discussion of the body is thus changed.

That gifts are given is clear, and Paul supports this with a quotation from Ps. 68:18. It is important that his quotation uses a word for gifts *(domata)* quite different from the one he used earlier. His earlier word *(charismata)* is not found in Ephesians or in Colossians at all. The emphasis has shifted even in the vocabulary used.

The list of gifts is more limited than previously. Each "gift" is a specific function in the church: apostles, prophets, evangelists, pastors, and teachers (Eph. 4:11). The impression is created that this is all there is to the church's worship activities, for at first sight it is *these* who equip the saints and build up the body. The enumeration of these functions comes close to the idea of "offices," an impression that is reinforced by the absence of other more inclusive gifts or functions. Two other features contribute to this same sense of exclusiveness: the repetitive "some," and the statement about the goal of these tasks "to equip the saints" (4:12). It is almost as if the body is divided into two in a way foreign to the description in I Corinthians: there are those who minister and those who are ministered to. A modification of this impression would be possible if the clause in 4:12 were punctuated, as is done in some recent editions, so that the persons listed in 4:11 do their work in order to equip the saints for the work of ministry and for the building up of the body of Christ (cf. Col. 3:16). Attractive as this possibility is, we cannot be sure this is what Paul meant. Even if correct, it is still true that Ephesians shows a considerable development of the idea of office through the distinction drawn between the general group of "saints" and the more responsible "ministry."

In Ephesians there is no list of *charismata* and no sense that everyone has a different gift. There is a heightened understanding of the church, and though it is possible that all still minister in some fashion or other, there is a greater degree of specificity in describing the functions of those who seem to be the core of the congregation.

This suggests that the church in Ephesus is more ordered, less charismatic, and more stable. Paul's concerns have shifted as the conditions have changed. The first blush of enthusiasm in the churches has faded. The need for a continuing organization is greater as the expectation of the end becomes more remote.

5. STAGE FOUR

It is relatively easy to see some additional developments as they are reflected in the pastoral letters, I and II Timothy, and Titus. It is difficult to imagine that Paul wrote these as they stand. There is a yet more developed "official" view of ministry in the church (e.g., I Tim. 3:1ff.; 3:8ff.; 4:6ff.; 4:14; 5:17ff.; 6:3ff.; 6:11ff.). A minister is set apart for special service, for which he is qualified by the laying on of hands. He is given authority to teach and pass on what he is given. The ethical demands for a church leader are more rigorous; his reputation is important; even his wife and children get special treatment. There can be little doubt that order is a primary preoccupation in the Pastorals.

Later, we can see in Ignatius' letters an even more restricted view. The bishop, by the year 110 or so, has become the *sole* representative of the church. The whole church revolves around him, so that it can do nothing without him. He is the symbol of the unity of the church and the one to whom everyone else defers.

6. CONCLUSION

That the sense of being a "church" developed over a period of sixty or so years is not remarkable. The de-emphasizing of freedom that goes along with it is important. The liberty to find new ways of adapting to new circumstances is still there —but those new ways of adapting, from the sixties on, seem to presuppose a restriction of the very liberty that gave rise to it. Adaptations and changes still take place, but they are in the direction of more order, more office-centered ministries. The liberty of the churches described in Acts and in Paul's letters, where the impact of the Spirit shows through clearly, alters. Part of this is a diminishing of awareness of the Spirit, part of it is a new set of needs when faced with the hostile impact of the outside world.

Whatever the reasons for the changes, it is abundantly clear that at some times and in some places there was a freedom in the church that must have seemed quite incredible against the Jewish background from which the church emerged. The sense of orderliness and dignity was shattered by the impact of the Spirit's new gifts that were to be shared in a corporate community context. So much was this the case that an appeal had to be made for more order and less confusion. As the church developed, the call for order became dominant, so that before long any theory of generally held *charismata* disappeared. Such gifts kept cropping up from time to time in the life of the church, but each time they were soon muted.

The church sometimes seems overconcerned for the orderly elements in its life and worship, though today we are witnessing a renewed emphasis on the gifts of the members of the community. Our attitude to this fresh movement today may well be affected by our understanding of the character of the early church. We should not neglect, then, the impression of enthusiasm, excitement, and vitality of some of Paul's churches as we seek to influence the character of ours.

VIII

Paul Today

PAUL IS always firmly rooted in his own religious inheritance. He frequently interacts with that inherited set of attitudes and assumptions. His interactions with his past views and practices are shot through with, indeed controlled by, his excitement over his faith in Jesus and his experience of the Spirit. Moreover, his immediate context is always in view. Whatever else one may say about Paul, one can never escape the complexity of the interpenetration of his immediate circumstances with his religious inheritance and his present religious experience.

Conversion is one word frequently applied to this relationship, but that suggests a more clear-cut distinction between his past and his present than is warranted. Paul was "converted," certainly, but this should be seen as conversion from Pharisaic Judaism to Messianic Judaism. Christianity is the result of the conversion of Paul; it is not the cause. Paul was, and remained, a Jew—a Jew absolutely persuaded of the unique messianic role of Jesus, of the atoning death of Jesus, and of the reality (and inevitability) of the experience of the Spirit who brings freedom.

1. PAUL AND FREEDOM

How important freedom was to Paul, and to him alone, can be seen from the following table of the use of the Greek words for "freedom," "free," and "to free," respectively:

		Lk/				Rest	Apost.
	Mk	Acts	Mt	Jn	Paul	of N.T.	Fathers
eleutheria	13	-	-	-	-	7	4	2
eleutheros	26	-	-	1	2	16	4	3
eleutheroō	8	-	-	-	2	5	-	1
	47	0	0	1	4	28	8	6

The New Testament occupies about twice as many pages as the Apostolic Fathers; Paul accounts for about one quarter of the New Testament. Of all this early Christian literature, Paul then accounts for about fifteen percent of the volume. Yet his use of "freedom" vocabulary accounts for sixty percent of the total use of words related to freedom. This simple statistical fact is an important indication of the role that freedom plays for Paul.

From the evidence we have we may draw the general conclusions that in early Christianity only Paul uses the notion of freedom with any degree of frequency. Within Paul's letter-writing activity it is the Paul of the earlier and middle period, rather than the later, who is characterized by the idea of freedom.

The phrase has been deliberately avoided up until now, but it is possible and, I think, correct to speak of Paul's *theology* of freedom. That theology has a theoretical basis, it has practical consequences in his own actions, and it leads to some difficult problems for him. It is only a partial exaggeration to say that Paul is the apostle of freedom, the only person in the whole of early Christianity, of whom we have literary evidence, who saw this side of the effect of Jesus. His achievement was spectacular.

It is in the hammering out of a basis for his theology of freedom that Paul is most creative. He has, one must admit, little to go on. He inherits traditions about Jesus in which Jesus' actions and words might lead to tentative conclusions about freedom, but little or no secure basis for it. It is primarily his reflection on the Hebrew Scriptures, illuminated by his view of Jesus and the implications of Jesus' death, that encouraged insights not imagined before. Secondarily, his own spiritual experience forced him to the view that God could do new things through his Spirit, who was himself present wherever Jesus was acknowledged as Lord.

Paul's creativity also may be seen in his ethical approach. Not only did he develop an important ethical principle—the principle of accommodation—in exciting directions, he also pointed to some extremely important ethical conclusions. The most notable was his comment that in Christ there is neither Jew nor Greek, slave nor free, male nor female. We saw reasons for his failure to carry this idea through fully, but that he even glimpsed the possibilities of overturning past practices is a tribute to this remarkable man. His ethical views were provocative and demanding, emphasizing regularly an inward motive for behavior that has stood up well in the test of time, even though it has not always been followed. Though he also was quite capable of commanding people's obedience, he expressed at other times an unwillingness to thus command. Then he was at his best.

However, this ability to encourage and support the fresh activities of the Spirit among the Christian believers led to trouble. Much of our treatment was predicated upon and illustrative of the problems that arose in Paul's churches.

Wherever freedom was encouraged, trouble followed, most obviously in Galatia and Corinth, to a lesser extent in Rome. The conflicts over freedom were one of the crucial debates in Paul's life, just as important as the debates over faith, apostleship, and Christology. His theology of freedom is real, pervasive, and extremely important. If Jesus means freedom (the title of a most illuminating book by Ernst Käsemann), Paul was the one—the only one—who claimed that freedom. Not only did he claim it for himself, he had the courage to claim it on behalf of the churches he founded.

It is not susceptible of proof, but I do not doubt that Paul operated on the basis of his claim to freedom all his life. In fact, it was his willingness to be free to all sorts of demands and for all sorts of people that led to his arrest and eventual death.

2. INTERPRETING PAUL'S FREEDOM TODAY

For those of us who take the Bible seriously, Paul's view of freedom poses an enormous challenge. Against a common view of Christianity which demonstrates little real freedom, his stress on it is an embarrassment. We do not know what to do with it. Most books on the New Testament and especially on Christian ethics give little indication of the place of freedom in Paul's thought.

At the same time the hints of development in Paul, and some sense of a diminution in freedom, are troubling also. Paul's views are not always the same; they vary with the occasion.

The development and change in Paul's theology is only a piece of a much larger development that occurs within the Bible as a whole. In part, that change is a result of a constantly changing context. The message of Scripture changes as the needs springing up from the circumstances change. In part, change is necessary because knowledge of God changes. What is said in the Psalms is different from what is said in Isaiah or Proverbs. The ethical advice of Deuteronomy differs from that of Amos, Daniel, or Revelation.

Paul's development is one facet of this process. He is an interpreter—an especially powerful interpreter—of the church's experience of the Holy Spirit, of Jesus as the Messiah and Lord, and of the Hebrew Scriptures as the revelation of God. He is different from earlier Jewish interpreters, who also were expositors of the Scriptures, with respect to his conviction that Jesus was the Messiah. He was different from contemporary Christian interpreters in his stress on the newness of the Spirit and the reality of the experience he brought. But basically Paul stands in the stream of tradition that links Moses, David, Isaiah, Habakkuk, John the Baptist, and Stephen, to name only a few. We might well have included also Hillel, Gamaliel, and the exegetes at Qumran in that same interpretive tradition. All wish to apply the Scriptures of the past to their changed present. As needs vary, interpretation and application vary. As a person's or a group's experiences vary, interpretation needs to be reworked. So Paul reinterprets the Hebrew Scriptures in the light of - the life and teaching and death and resurrection and Lordship of Jesus, under the impact of the Holy Spirit. Such a reinterpretation of Scripture might seem at first sight to be unprincipled. It is not. Instead, it values consistency less than reality and applicability. It is a principle of accommodation.

We cannot afford the luxury of simply selecting one side or other of Paul. We shall have to interpret Paul in some appropriate way for ourselves, in the light of our circumstances. A first step is to recognize that our use of Paul (and the rest of Scripture) should be analogous to Paul's use of Scripture. That is, just as Paul's view of freedom is a reinterpretation of the Old Testament in the light of Jesus and of the Holy Spirit, and just as Jesus is an interpreter of the prophets, and just as the prophets are interpreters of the law, so we are interpreters of the message of Paul. The applicational and interpretive need is similar. This is not to deny that the Scriptural canon is closed. It is clear that our reinterpretations of Scripture will never themselves become Scripture. Scripture remains the norm and standard. But it is not always directly capable of being applied to circumstances that are radically different—socially, culturally, religiously, politically. Especially is this the case when the question at issue is a matter in which, as with freedom, the context is to a large extent determinative of the approach.

To take an example from recent history, the Christians who argued for the abolition of slavery did so through an interpretation of Paul for their own day against the evils of an institution that had changed greatly from Paul's day. His writings did not give a simple answer. There was no injunction to abolish slavery lurking in Scripture and overlooked for eighteen hundred years. Nevertheless, their conclusion that slavery was abhorrent was based on Paul. Their application can now be seen to be quite correct, even though those who defended slavery because it was presupposed by Scripture were more literally correct. There was a word from the Lord about slavery in the 1800's, precisely because sensitive Christians saw that there was a legitimate kind of freedom in applying Scripture intelligently and appropriately to changed circumstances. I would call this "hermeneutical freedom," that is, the freedom—demand might be a better word—to take the development and change in Scripture as indicative of the freedom to apply the word of the Lord to specific circumstances in different ways. We should presuppose the same kind of interpretive freedom today, while still remaining tied to Scripture.

I select three issues for brief comment as indicative of ways in which Paul's freedom might apply today.

a. Women

The subjugation of women needs no documentation. The roots of that view in Paul's letters are strikingly apparent and have influenced Christian thinking since. Though Paul was not the male chauvinist he has been made out to be by critics, neither was he free from all accusations leveled at him. It is certain that Paul accepted women's roles in church worship at least with respect to certain acts such as praying and prophesying. It is likely that he actively encouraged those actions at least at one stage in his ministry. If he later relaxed his position, as I think likely, because trouble arose in the churches on account of that assertion of freedom, it would seem that his basic insight still stands. Our situation is marked by an enormous increase in the variety and importance of the roles that women fill, from controlling the family budget to being President or Prime Minister. That change should encourage us to seize upon and apply the basic conviction of Paul: in Christ there is neither male nor female. Hermeneutical freedom, interacting with one facet of Paul's view of freedom, allows us to transcend nineteen hundred years of injustice and, as with slavery, to call for a completely liberated view of women.

Paul's injunctions to subordination, which we should not overlook or dismiss from the text, are marked by a quality of defensiveness characteristic of an embattled disputant. Paul's concern for subordinating women is partly exegetical, partly cultural, and partly practical. In his struggles and conflicts it became easier for him to retreat from one of his earlier claims. As we seek to interpret Scripture *our* exegetical, cultural, and practical insights need also to play a part. If it is fair to pose a hypothetical question, Would Paul today

be on the side of the Equal Rights Amendment? I believe he
would.

b. Church and Ministry

The changing direction of Paul's thoughts on the church
pointed toward a more structured view of the church and a
limited form of ministry. In fact, this was the direction in
which the church, in time, moved. But the contrast between
those later developed forms and what Paul says in I Corinthians, in particular, is stark. Do we take the actual development seriously, or some earlier view that was later superseded?

Paul's earlier view, expressed most fully in I Corinthians,
is one that resonates with the need for a revitalization of the
church today. The often stereotyped views of the distinction
between clergy and laity, the rigidity of forms of worship, the
impersonal relationships between Christians in the same congregation, all conflict with some of Paul's descriptions. Conversely, the emphasis on the church as a body, with all its
parts building together into a single whole, the emphasis on
the manner in which persons are given gifts by the Spirit, and
the emphasis on specific contributions all draw extra meaning from today's awareness of the importance of personal
relationships and group activity. These are the features
through which the early church gave evidence of freedom. It
should be no surprise that many today are looking for that
same freedom within the church.

To stress today such a "Corinthian" view of the church
would require a downplaying of the later developments. Is
this legitimate hermeneutically? I think it is, on the basis that
those later views represent a view concerned for meeting
challenges. It is a part of that later "legalizing" of the church
that sets in gradually as the church's experience of the Spirit
wanes. Our situation is different; with hundreds of years of

minimal participation by the ordinary church member we need to recover the interrelatedness of the church. Paul's body concept allows for this.

c. Accommodation Ethics

Our generation has witnessed the rise and fall of "situation ethics." We still seem regularly faced with some simple contrast between an ethic of prescription and one with little or no substance. Paul's view of accommodation—to be all things to all men—has become synonymous with not having any standards whatsoever. It is now a slur, equivalent to being wishy-washy. But it should not be so viewed. It represents Paul's most considered response to the challenge of ethics, a view concerned not for oneself but for the good of others. Whatever Paul did was always aimed toward the goal of winning some to the Lord.

In our ethical situation today, we should give serious attention to this notion which allows for a genuine sense of freedom, a concern for the other, a dominant principle of love, and a building up of the body. These are desperately needed within the church and Paul's statements provide a starting point for a better ethical approach today. The church's past has been far too much concerned for the "new law" approach that crept in quickly. In so doing, it led the church away from its primary resources, the new inwardness of the Spirit.

3. Conclusion

Each of these examples—women, church, and ethics—is an area in which the church over the years has not come up to Paul's best insights. We should develop a hermeneutic that allows us to take seriously Paul's view of freedom in these areas. We should do so not simply because we prefer these views of his to others but because the conditions that called forth these insights still apply today. As we understand the needs and problems of our day, we should be able to return to Scripture to find fresh resources for the challenges that face us.

Paul develops a theology of freedom that touches our needs closely. Its features are still powerful—a stress on the Spirit, personal responsibility, the corporateness of the Christian community, the mutuality of male and female. We can change with the assurance that "Christ has set us free for freedom."

Bibliography

FOOTNOTES have been deliberately avoided as unnecessary for scholars and irksome to others. My own understanding of Paul has been greatly enriched by studies too numerous and too technical to be of interest to the general reader.

The following list is intended to be of use to persons who have nontechnical interests in the further study of Paul. I have avoided suggesting books that presuppose a knowledge of Greek or Hebrew, although some of the following books make use of non-English words occasionally. Written from a variety of perspectives, all are in some sense careful, critically based studies of Paul.

Bornkamm, Günther, *Paul.* Harper & Row, Publishers, 1971.

Bruce, F. F., *The Letters of Paul: An Expanded Paraphrase.* Wm. B. Eerdmans Publishing Co., 1965.

Davies, W. D., *Paul and Rabbinic Judaism.* 3d ed. London: S.P.C.K., 1970.

Deissmann, Adolf, *Paul: A Study in Social and Religious History.* 1927. Reprint. Harper & Brothers, 1957.

Drane, John W., *Paul: Libertine or Legalist?* London: S.P.C.K., 1975.

Ellis, E. Earle, *Paul and His Recent Interpreters.* Wm. B. Eerdmans Publishing Co., 1961.

Hanson, A. T., *Studies in Paul's Technique and Theology.*
London: S.P.C.K., 1974.

Hurd, John C., Jr., *The Origin of I Corinthians.* Seabury
Press, 1965.

Käsemann, Ernst, *Perspectives on Paul.* London: SCM Press,
1971.

Longenecker, Richard N., *Paul: Apostle of Liberty.* 1964.
Reprint. Baker Book House, 1976.

Munck, Johannes, *Paul and the Salvation of Mankind.* London: SCM Press, 1959.

Roetzel, Calvin J., *The Letters of Paul.* John Knox Press,
1975.

Schoeps, H. J., *Paul: The Theology of the Apostle in the Light
of Jewish Religious History.* Westminster Press, 1961.

Stendahl, Krister, *Paul Among Jews and Gentiles.* Fortress
Press, 1976.

Whiteley, D. E. H., *The Theology of St. Paul.* Oxford: Basil
Blackwell, Publisher, 1964.

Index of Passages Cited

Index of Subjects

DATE DUE

8 07. '80	
10. 09. '80	
2 19 '81	
12 03. '81	
6. 10. '82	
5. 31 '84	
5 16 '85	
5 30 '85	
5 4 '86	
APR 18 '86	
FEB 24 '93	
rtn. 3/7